Roadmap to Federal Jobs

How to Determine Your Qualifications, Develop an Effective USAJOBS Resume, Apply for and Land U.S. Government Jobs

CareerPro Global
YOUR CAREER IS OUR BUSINESS®

CAREERPRO GLOBAL, INC.
173 Pierce Avenue
Macon, GA 31204

Printed in the United States of America
Roadmap to Federal Jobs: How to Determine Your Qualifications, Develop an Effective USAJOBS Resume, Apply for and Land U.S. Government Jobs

ISBN: 978-0-9823222-3-9

Copyright © 2018 by CareerPro Global, Inc.

CareerPro Global's 21st-Century Career Series

Publication Team:

Interior Page Design/Layout: Patricia Duckers
Cover Design: Alesha Sevy-Kelley
Proofreading: Carla Lowe
Contributors: William Porter, Michelle Czyz, William Carroll, Heather Gant, Ted Telega, Patricia Duckers

Disclaimer: The information, tips, best practices, and resources in this book are based on several decades of experience in the career management industry, but individual experiences and results will vary, and depend solely on your efforts. While CareerPro Global gladly shares this information to assist you, we can in no way be held responsible for the results in your own job search. In addition, the sample resumes are adapted from and based on actual clients, but the names, dates, organizations, and many other details and specifics have been fictionalized to protect individual privacy. The information published in this book is accurate at the time of printing; however, over time, some of the information may change, and CareerPro Global is not responsible for any of these changes.

About the Authors

Barbara Adams has led CareerPro Global, Inc. (CPG) for almost three decades, and has built CPG into one of the largest and fastest-growing career services organizations industry-wide, having served more than 60,000 clients to date. Barbara positioned CPG to raise the bar by developing an ISO 9001:2008-guided quality process (the first in the careers industry) through which all of CPG's processes were reviewed and measured for quality. CPG held full ISO 9001:2008 certification/registration from 2010 to 2017, and still maintains an internal quality control system based on those standards.

Barbara earned the Career Innovation Award for this implementation and focus on quality of workmanship, process, and people. Barbara has also co-authored several books in CareerPro's 21st-Century Career Series, including *Roadmap to the Senior Executive Service, Roadmap to Job-Winning Military to Civilian Resumes,* and *Roadmap to Becoming an Administrative Law Judge.* Barbara employs some of the best—if not the best—writers and career advisers in the industry and provides ongoing training in support of hiring trends and protocol. CareerPro Global is one of the most trusted career management services in the industry.

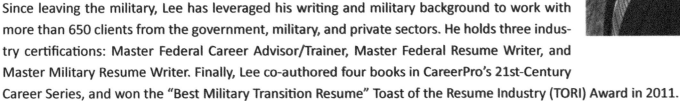

Lee Kelley is the senior member of CPG's writing team, and serves on the executive staff as Director of Training and Managing Editor for over a dozen other writers. He is also a veteran who spent 10 years in the U.S. Army, working his way from Private to Captain. He spent a year in Ramadi, Iraq (2005–2006) in support of Operation Iraqi Freedom, and his last position in the Army was Commanding Officer of a 275-person headquarters organization.

Since leaving the military, Lee has leveraged his writing and military background to work with more than 650 clients from the government, military, and private sectors. He holds three industry certifications: Master Federal Career Advisor/Trainer, Master Federal Resume Writer, and Master Military Resume Writer. Finally, Lee co-authored four books in CareerPro's 21st-Century Career Series, and won the "Best Military Transition Resume" Toast of the Resume Industry (TORI) Award in 2011.

About CareerPro Global, Inc.

In business since 1986, CPG offers world-class services in resume writing, career coaching, onsite career training, career publications, and webinar-based training. Our multi-credentialed Master Writers and Career Advisors are some of the best—if not the best—in the careers industry. Our team members specialize in corporate, military, and federal clients seeking to stand out in a competitive job market. They are published authors, journalists, editors, branding experts, Human Resources (HR) professionals, engineers, Information Technology (IT) professionals, educators, public-relations professionals, and veterans from both the enlisted and officer ranks. Our track record of setting industry standards has been attributed to our methodology, delivery, and commitment to excellence. Utilizing our expertise, thousands of clients across all fields and professional levels have succeeded in reaching their career goals.

Our Mission Statement: At CareerPro Global, we are committed to producing premier resume and career services products, providing service excellence, hiring talented professionals, and remaining abreast of global employment and hiring trends. We are also committed to continuous improvement of the quality management system.

Books, Articles, Publications, and Media: CareerPro Global and its team members have created/published 300+ online and print articles relating to career coaching, resume writing, job searching, interview skills, and salary negotiations, and has published the following titles:

- Roadmap to the Senior Executive Service
- Roadmap to Job-Winning Military to Civilian Resumes
- Roadmap to Becoming an Administrative Law Judge
- Roadmap to Federal Jobs
- Roadmap to the Senior Executive Service – 2nd Edition

Quality Management System: CPG's culture has been built upon, and remains committed to, our core factors, which include: honesty, integrity, excellent customer service, and a passion for helping others achieve their career goals. We believe so strongly in these core factors that our company has raised the bar by developing a Quality Management System, where all our processes are reviewed for quality.

Longevity and Success: CPG combines three decades of industry writing experience with the most advanced technology in the industry, empowering us to produce job-winning resume presentations for our clients. We also pride ourselves in producing results and outstanding customer service. And it shows. We hold a 99.6% customer satisfaction ratio. These statistics are backed up by our monthly customer service survey and ongoing commitment to delivering quality products and services.

Research, Development, and Systems: CPG is extremely proactive in research and development. Investing in our own in-house Information Technology department has given us the capability to ensure secure transaction processing and data warehousing. CPG developed and utilizes one of the most robust system architectures in the industry, integrating and customizing portfolios of collaborative and communication services designed to connect people, information, processes, and systems, both within and beyond our firewall.

Training, Certification, and Industry Excellence:
- Authored and administer: MFCA (Master Federal Career Advisor)

- Authored and administer: MFCA/T (Master Federal Career Advisor/Trainer)
- Authored and administer: MMRW (Master Military Resume Writer)
- Authored and administer MSEW (Master Senior Executive Writer)
- Authored and administer MFRW-T (Master Federal Resume Writer/Trainer)
- Launched new in-house SES SOPs for Senior Executive Service
- Authored and administer Master Federal Resume Writer (MFRW)
- Industry experts and mentors in military, federal, and civilian resumes
- Recognized as industry leaders and innovators
- Career conference presenters and speakers
- Webinar presenters on resume topics
- Innovation Award, Careers Industry
- Seven TORI (Toast of the Resume Industry) nominations
- Winner, Best Military Transition Resume (Toast of the Resume Industry)

Holders of the following certifications:
- Certified Professional Resume Writer (CPRW)
- Certified Advanced Resume Writer (CARW)
- Certified Expert Resume Writer (CERW)
- Certified Electronic Career Coach (CECC)
- Master Military Resume Writer (MMRW)
- Master Federal Resume Writer (MFRW)
- Master Federal Career Advisor – Trainer (MFCA - T)
- Certified Employment Interview Coach (CEIC)
- Master Senior Executive Writer (MSEW)

This book is dedicated to all current and future government employees who share their time, talents, and dedication to improve quality of life for all American citizens.

TABLE OF CONTENTS

CD-ROM CONTENTS

Worksheets and Customizable Samples:

- Accomplishments Worksheet
- Cover Letter Sample
- KSA Worksheet
- Roadmap to Federal Jobs Worksheet
- Traditional Federal Resume Template (for uploading)
- USAJOBS Resume Builder

Resume Samples:

- Federal GS-13: Aviation Safety Inspector
- Federal GS-13: Security Specialist
- Military to GS-5: Human Resources
- Military to GS-7: Veterans Service Representative
- Military to GS-12: HR Specialist/Program Analyst
- Military to GS-12: Intelligence Analyst
- Military to GS-15: Supervisory Program Management
- Private Sector to GS-7: Dental Hygienist
- Private Sector to GS-9: Program Specialist
- Private Sector to GS-11: Linguist/Foreign Language Instructor
- Private Sector to GS-15: Land/Property Management
- Private Sector to WG-12: Aircraft Mechanic

SYMBOLS

You'll notice the following graphics throughout the book. Think of them as signposts along your roadmap, offering best practices and other useful information to guide your learning experience and career journey.

 **PRACTICAL EXERCISES**

 **DECISION TIME**

 **SAMPLES**

 **BEST PRACTICES**

 **CPG EXCLUSIVE**

 **TAKE NOTE**

UNDERSTANDING THE FEDERAL JOB LANDSCAPE

WHY WORK FOR THE GOVERNMENT?

The federal government is the largest employer in the U.S., with more than 2.8M employees at its peak. For the decade between 2007 and 2018, there were often as many as 20K job openings at any given time. Despite turbulent times, such as government furloughs, and then a hiring freeze in early 2017, the U.S. federal government still has roughly two million employees, and thousands of positions will need to be filled as people retire, move around, or leave government service for whatever reason.

If we look back over time and keep the larger picture in mind, it's clear that the federal government has long been a wonderful career path for a diverse workforce of millions of Americans.

After helping people enter and move around within the federal government for more than 30 years, CareerPro Global believes that even if there are short-term cuts and cultural changes, the government will continue to offer highly attractive career opportunities for those seeking public service.

Our clients each have their own reasons and motivations for joining the government, but a few primary themes have emerged over the years:

- A sense of workplace security
- Career ladders, promotions, and transfer opportunities
- An Equal Employment Opportunity (EEO) workplace
- The honor of public service to our great nation
- Benefits packages
- Retirement benefits
- Federal holidays
- Paid vacation, family, and medical leave
- Travel opportunities
- Training and professional development

Here are more details on some of the many benefits available. Additional benefits and perks may vary, according to agency and position.

Federal Employees Health Benefits Program (FEHB)

The government's health benefits program offers approximately 180 health plan options throughout the United States (U.S.), including consumer-driven health-care and preferred provider network options. On the average, every employee has at least a dozen plan choices, each with varying benefits. None of the federal health plans requires a waiting period or a medical exam for enrollment.

Dental and Vision Insurance

Dental and vision benefits are available to eligible federal and postal employees, retirees, and their eligible family members on an enrollee-pay-all basis. This program allows dental insurance to be purchased on a group basis, which means competitive premiums and no pre-existing condition limitations. Premiums for enrolled federal and postal employees are withheld from salary on a pre-tax basis.

Flexible Spending Accounts (FSAs)

FSAs allow employees to increase their disposable income because the amounts they contribute are not subject to federal income, FICA, or state or local income taxes. The federal government offers both a Healthcare FSA and a Dependent Care FSA. Employees can use the Healthcare FSA for expenses that are tax-deductible, but not reimbursed by any other source, including out-of-pocket expenses and non-covered benefits under their FEHB plans.

Some examples are non-covered dental services, LASIK surgery, health plan deductibles, and co-payments and coinsurance. Dependent Care FSAs are available for employees with dependent children or qualifying dependent adults when the care is necessary to allow the employee to work.

Leave and Holidays

Federal employees are entitled to at least 13 days of vacation leave as well as 13 days of sick leave each year. Depending on years of service, employees can earn up to 26 days of vacation leave each year. In addition, federal employees are entitled to 10 days of paid holiday each year. The rate of a new employee's annual leave accrual rate may be negotiable when an applicant receives a job offer.

Family-Friendly Flexibilities

The federal government provides many programs for workers to support their needs for individual flexibility. For example, Compressed Work Schedules allow employees to adjust their work hours in order to take a day off each pay period.

Employees can enjoy 26 three-day weekends! Further, the federal government's Alternative Work Schedule (AWS) allows employees to select certain arrival and departure times that best suit their needs within their working day; this is often known as "flextime" (flexible time). Individual agencies have policies regarding family-friendly work schedules.

Federal Employees Retirement System (FERS)

A federal employee's retirement benefits are based on years of service and salary history.

Thrift Savings Plan (TSP)

With the Thrift Savings Plan [similar to a 401(k) plan], an employee can self-direct his/her retirement savings program through multiple investment options.

Social Security

Federal employees hired beginning in (and beyond) 1984 and covered under the Federal Employee Retirement System (FERS) earn Social Security credit while working with the government.

Retirement

New employees with previous government service prior to 1984 may be eligible to participate in the Civil Service Retirement System (CSRS). Employees in law enforcement-designated positions are covered under a separate retirement system; certain other positions may offer alternative retirement program options, as well.

Medicare - Part A

Government employees are automatically eligible for Medicare - Part A at no cost, beginning at age 65.

Federal Employees' Group Life Insurance (FEGLI)

FEGLI is a group term life insurance program. It consists

of basic life insurance coverage and three options. In most cases, new federal employees are automatically covered by basic life insurance. There are three additional forms of optional insurance from which an employee can choose, including: Standard, Additional, and Family.

Long-Term Care Insurance Program

All new employees and their family members are eligible to apply for long-term care insurance under the Federal Long Term Care Insurance Program (FLTCIP) with minimal underwriting.

Recruitment Incentives

Certain new federal hires may be eligible for recruitment incentives, which are traditionally paid to people appointed to difficult-to-fill positions. The availability of a recruitment incentive should be on the vacancy announcement.

Relocation Incentives

In some cases, the government will provide eligible applicants with a one-time incentive to relocate to a geographic area where it has had difficulty attracting qualified applicants. This varies from a relocation allowance, which some agencies give to qualified candidates to assist them with their relocation expenses.

Incentive Awards

These include: Monetary, Time Off, Honorary, and nonmonetary, and are given to recognize exceptional accomplishments and/or contributions made on the job.

Employee Development

Federal employees have a myriad of professional enrichment options available to them. These opportunities ensure the employees continue to grow and adapt to the changing needs of their jobs.

Supportive of Community Service

Community leadership is encouraged by the government; as such, the annual Combined Federal Campaign (CFC) provides federal employees an opportunity to contribute to various charities.

Interagency Transfers

Employees in the Competitive Service positions may transfer from one federal agency/position to another without a break in service or seniority.

Student Loan Repayment

Depending on the agency's policies, eligible employees may receive reimbursement for their student loans. This reimbursement is generally granted if the employee went to school for a specific program that is usually hard for the government to fill, but it's also determined on a case-by-case basis.

Some benefits—such as starting salary, annual leave, and recruitment incentives, to name just a few—are negotiable. New entrants to the Federal Service should enquire about the availability of such options prior to accepting a position. Generally, benefits are available to employees who are appointed to positions for a duration of more than one year.

With all this in mind, we sincerely hope that you'll consider sharing some of your own talents and serving in our government so that it can continue to provide much-needed services and support to our nation's citizens.

How Much Can You Earn?

In the past decade, the average salary for federal employees has grown, and according to the U.S. Bureau of Economic Analysis (BEA), in 2016, federal civilian workers had an average wage of $88,809. That's more than $20K higher than the average wage among the country's 114 million private-sector workers.

When you start applying to specific job announcements, you'll notice that the salary is represented by a range.

Federal compensation is based on several factors. In the Competitive Service, pay is based on the level and nature of the work to be performed. If the work is considered "Grade 9-level work," then an applicant will be paid at the grade 9 level, regardless of experience, skills, or education.

Pay scales are also adjusted by geographic location, so the general pay scale in New York City will be higher than the pay scale in Montana. Just remember that regardless of location, the position would still be considered a Grade 9. Special pay rates and different scales also vary by location and grade (this applies to engineers, for example). Additionally, the Office of Personnel Management (OPM) has the authority to establish higher rates of basic pay, called special rates, for a group or category of General Schedule (GS) positions in one or more geographic areas to address existing or likely significant handicaps in recruiting or retaining well-qualified employees.

According to the Partnership for Public Service, "the General Schedule (GS) is the predominant pay scale for federal employees, especially employees in professional, technical, administrative or clerical positions. The system consists of 15 grades, from GS-1, the lowest level, to GS-15, the highest level. There are also 10 steps within each grade. The grade level assigned to a position determines the pay level for that job."

For instance, GS-3 or GS-4 is typically used for internships or student jobs:

- GS-5 to GS-7 represents mostly entry-level positions
- GS-8 to GS-12 represents mid-level positions
- GS-13 to GS-15 represents the top-level supervisory positions
- Any positions beyond GS-15 are part of the Senior Executive Service (SES), an elite level of government leadership that falls just below political appointment.

The table below represents the national minimum for the GS levels 1-15 as of January 1, 2018. Please note that federal pay scales are adjusted annually.

INCORPORATING THE 1.4% GENERAL SCHEDULE INCREASE
EFFECTIVE JANUARY 2018

Annual Rates by Grade and Step

Grade	Step 1	Step 2	Step 3	Step 4	Step 5	Step 6	Step 7	Step 8	Step 9	Step 10	WITHIN GRADE AMOUNTS
1	$ 18,785	$ 19,414	$ 20,039	$ 20,660	$ 21,285	$ 21,650	$ 22,267	$ 22,891	$ 22,915	$ 23,502	VARIES
2	21,121	21,624	22,323	22,915	23,175	23,857	24,539	25,221	25,903	26,585	VARIES
3	23,045	23,813	24,581	25,349	26,117	26,885	27,653	28,421	29,189	29,957	768
4	25,871	26,733	27,595	28,457	29,319	30,181	31,043	31,905	32,767	33,629	862
5	28,945	29,910	30,875	31,840	32,805	33,770	34,735	35,700	36,665	37,630	965
6	32,264	33,339	34,414	35,489	36,564	37,639	38,714	39,789	40,864	41,939	1,075
7	35,854	37,049	38,244	39,439	40,634	41,829	43,024	44,219	45,414	46,609	1,195
8	39,707	41,031	42,355	43,679	45,003	46,327	47,651	48,975	50,299	51,623	1,324
9	43,857	45,319	46,781	48,243	49,705	51,167	52,629	54,091	55,553	57,015	1,462
10	48,297	49,907	51,517	53,127	54,737	56,347	57,957	59,567	61,177	62,787	1,610
11	53,062	54,831	56,600	58,369	60,138	61,907	63,676	65,445	67,214	68,983	1,769
12	63,600	65,720	67,840	69,960	72,080	74,200	76,320	78,440	80,560	82,680	2,120
13	75,628	78,149	80,670	83,191	85,712	88,233	90,754	93,275	95,796	98,317	2,521
14	89,370	92,349	95,328	98,307	101,286	104,265	107,244	110,223	113,202	116,181	2,979
15	105,123	108,627	112,131	115,635	119,139	122,643	126,147	129,651	133,155	136,659	3,504

Federal Wage System (FWS)

The Federal Wage System (FWS) is a uniform pay-setting system that covers federal-appropriated fund and non-appropriated fund blue-collar employees who are paid by the hour, and is typically most used by the Department of Defense (DOD), although other agencies, such as the Department of Veterans Affairs (VA), also have Wage Grade (WG) employees.

The system's goal is to ensure federal trade, craft, and laboring employees, within a local wage area and who perform the same duties, receive the same rate of pay.

Under this uniform pay system, you can expect your pay to be the generally same as the pay of other federal jobs like theirs in your wage area as well as be in line with pay for private-sector jobs like yours.

Pay Bands

Some agencies, such as the Transportation Security Administration (or TSA, part of the Department of Homeland Security, or DHS) use a Pay Banding System. As such, positions within the TSA do not start with the "GS" designation like the General Schedule positions; rather, their prefix is "SV."

The primary differences between the GS and SV pay schedules is that SV is much more basic. There's a minimum salary and a maximum salary, with no clearly defined steps in between.

Further, instead of being assigned a numeric value, as is done with the GS series—e.g., GS-2210-14—Pay Banding assigns a letter, A through M, to designate the different pay levels.

Other Types of Compensation

In addition to the pay schedules previously listed, there are other scales, including that which is used for the Se-

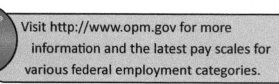

Visit http://www.opm.gov for more information and the latest pay scales for various federal employment categories.

nior Executive Service (SES) and non-competitive positions, such as Administrative Law Judges (ALJs), Law Enforcement Specialists, Executives, Members of Boards of Contract Appeals, and Employees in Senior-Level (SL) and Scientific and Professional (ST) positions.

Each agency and vacancy will have different requirements in determining what constitutes the different pay bands and ranges. Additional information about converting government pay bands to the more typical grades can usually be found in job announcements under "Qualifications."

The following is a list of some additional federal pay systems:

- AL (Administrative Law Judge)
- ES (Senior Executive Service)
- EX (Executive Schedule)
- GG (General Grade)
- SL (Senior-Level positions)
- ST (Scientific and Professional positions)
- SV (Transportation Security Administration)
- VN (Department of Veterans Affairs nurses)

What Kinds of Jobs Are Available?

Just as there is a need to classify the separate vocations of the private-sector workforce [e.g., Information Technology (IT), Finance, and Security professionals, etc.], the same need exists in the federal government.

The federal government assigns a numeric classification system to its occupational groups, which include the General Schedule (typically reserved for what are called "white-collar" positions in the private sector) and the WG groups for "blue-collar" workers.

Job Categories, Eligibility, & Special Programs

All federal jobs fall under one of the following "categories": Competitive Service, Excepted Service, and Direct Hire. Let's delve a little deeper into each one.

Competitive Service

Competitive Service covers jobs that fall solely under the Office of Personnel Management's (OPM) jurisdiction and that are subject to the Civil Service laws passed by Congress to ensure applicants and employees receive fair and equal treatment in the hiring process.

Candidates are chosen from an applicant pool based on their qualifications and how closely they meet the desired knowledge, skills, abilities, and competencies stated in the vacancy announcement.

Competitive Service jobs cover a significant percentage of federal employment opportunities. The objective is to identify the best-qualified candidates for the vacancy.

Applicants typically consist of people from the private sector, the federal employment ranks, and former military service personnel who are attempting to transition to post-military employment. Only U.S. citizens are eligible for positions in the Competitive Service.

Most agencies under the federal government fall under Competitive Service, although some agencies have both Competitive and Excepted Service positions.

Excepted Service (Direct Hire)

While the vast majority of the agencies list their vacancies through USAJOBS.gov (and their employment links will redirect you to this site), some positions are "excepted" by law because the agencies have direct ties to national security and/or intelligence functions, or are otherwise inappropriate for competitive examining.

Candidates interested in these types of position should consult the official website of the agencies that offer this type of employment opportunity. Here is a partial list of agencies offering non-competitive employment opportunities:

- Administrative Office of the U.S. Courts
- Central Intelligence Agency (CIA)
- Department of Transportation (DOT)
- Federal Aviation Administration (FAA)
- Federal Air Marshal Service (FAMS)
- Defense Intelligence Agency (DIA)
- Federal Bureau of Investigation (FBI)
- U.S. Department of Justice (DOJ)
- U.S. Secret Service-Uniformed Division (USSS)
- Federal Reserve Board
- Government Accountability Office (GAO)
- Military Sealift Command (MSC)
- National Geospatial-Intelligence Agency (NGA)
- National Security Agency (NSA)
- National Science Foundation (NSF)
- Nuclear Regulatory Commission (NRC)
- Peace Corps
- Tennessee Valley Authority (TVA)
- United States Postal Service (USPS)
- Federal Reserve System, Board of Governors
- United States Agency for International Development (USAID)
- Department of Veterans Affairs (VA)—mostly Veterans Healthcare Administration health-allied positions
- U.S. Department of State

Federal Hiring Paths

Explore Hiring Paths

The Federal Government offers unique hiring paths (also known as a hiring authority) to help hire individuals that represent our diverse society. If you fall under one of these groups of people you may be eligible to receive preference when applying for jobs.

Open to the Public
Never worked for the Federal Government, U.S. citizens or nationals

Federal Employees
Current or former

Veterans

National Guard & Reserves
Current or prospective members

Individuals with a disability

Native Americans
American Indian or Alaskan Native

Military Spouses

Students & Recent Graduates

Senior Executives

Peace Corps/VISTA Alumni

Family of overseas employees
Family members

- U.S. Supreme Court, Personnel Office
- National Maritime Intelligence Center
- U.S. Department of Homeland Security, Transportation Security Administration
- Department of Defense Education Activity (DoDEA)
- Naval Acquisition Career Center or Naval Acquisition Intern Program
- National Nuclear Security Administration (NNS

Open to the Public

Learn more about how U.S. citizens and nationals can apply for thousands of jobs that are open to the public on the USAJOBS.gov homepage.

Federal Employees

Current or former federal employees may be able to apply for certain Competitive Service positions under merit promotion consideration. Find out more on the USAJOBS.gov homepage.

Veterans

Veterans who served on Active Duty and separated under honorable conditions may get Veterans' Preference and other veteran-centric hiring options. Find out more in Checkpoint 7 and on the USAJOBS.gov homepage.

Military Spouses

The federal government has a non-competitive process to help military spouses land both temporary and permanent jobs. You can learn more on the USAJOBS.gov homepage.

National Guard and Reserve

Whether you're already in the National Guard or the Reserve, or willing to join, you can find out more about eligibility on the USAJOBS.gov homepage under hiring paths.

Individuals with a Disability

Not only can people with disabilities apply for any job for which they are eligible, but they may also get special hiring authority. Find more information about programs and eligibility requirements on the USAJOBS.gov homepage.

Native Americans

You might be eligible for "Indian Preference" if you're an American Indian or an Alaskan Native who is a member of one of the federally recognized tribes. Find much more information about programs and eligibility requirements on the USAJOBS.gov homepage.

Students and Recent Graduates

Current students and recent graduates may be eligible for federal internships and jobs through the Pathways program and other student programs. Find much more information about programs and eligibility requirements on the USAJOBS.gov homepage.

Senior Executive Service

(See Checkpoint 8 starting on page 91.)

Peace Corps/VISTA alumni

If you served with the Peace Corps or AmeriCorps Volunteers in Service to America (VISTA) program, you may qualify for non-competitive eligibility.

This means that a federal agency can hire you outside of the formal competitive job announcement process. Find more information about programs and eligibility requirements on the USAJOBS.gov homepage.

Family of Overseas Employees

If you're currently overseas with a family member, and moving back to the U.S., you may be eligible for a Competitive Service job without having to compete with the public.

In addition, if you're moving overseas because a family member has been assigned to an overseas duty of station, you may be eligible to apply for overseas jobs

with the federal government. Find more information about programs and eligibility requirements on the USAJOBS.gov homepage.

Susan's Story

As we guide you through the steps that you must follow to find, prepare for, and land federal jobs, we will use a case study for "Susan Jackson." Susan's name, resume details, and other facts have been fictionalized, but she represents many similar customers whom we have assisted over the years.

Susan majored in Communications at the University of Montana before entering corporate America as a Public Affairs Specialist and later becoming an Outreach Director for a medium-sized logistics company. Susan has decided that in the political and social environments of 2018, she would like to enter the federal workforce and do her part in making improvements from the inside.

She's interested in targeting writing/editing or Congressional/Public Affairs positions at the GS-9 to 11 level. Susan's old resume, before she learned the best practices in this book, begins on the next page.

Susan Jackson

123 Sparse Lane, Ogden, UT 84559 | Phone: 123-456-7890 | Email: susan@gmail.com

Country of Citizenship:	United States of America
Veterans' Preference:	N/A
Job Type:	Permanent
Work Schedule:	Full Time

PROFESSIONAL EXPERIENCE

Outreach Director   2013-Present
Global Logistics   Hours per week: 60

Responsible for planning, managing, and administering government relations programs for both small and large technology industry clients doing business with multiple agencies. Develops and executes legislative strategies for corporations seeking to influence the Congress. One of the top 3 firm members specializing in DOD to Congress relations. Provides expert advice to both small and large Defense technology industry clients to help them navigate the complex Congressional oversight and appropriations processes.

- Developed short-term strategies for smaller clients designed to impact Congressional decisions on broad-ranging topics from tax initiatives to research, development, test, and evaluation focus areas.
- Conducted research; analyzed and provided important legislative information and technical advice to major corporations.
- Designed, planned, and implemented strategies for establishing and maintaining communications with Members of Congress, key committees, and their staffs.
- Guided smaller, innovative technology companies through the maze of Executive Branch agencies providing critical information on documented requirements.
- Leveraged Congressional oversight to convince the National Oceanic and Atmospheric Administration to begin purchasing commercially available satellite atmospheric data.
- Prepared several senior corporate executives and chief executive officers of client companies for testimony before the House Appropriations Committee. Tailored the client's written and spoken testimony to achieve strategy objectives. Coached the witnesses to prepare them for the hearing. In every case, the impact of the testimony was effective and beneficial to the client's cause.
- Drafted and/or reviewed hundreds of reports and correspondence to members of Congress and Congressional Committees for clients; often working with DOD agencies to help review Congressional engagement to synchronize with supporting industry.
- Represented client corporations at Congressional events and meetings with Members of Congress and their staff. Scheduled, orchestrated, and attended meetings with Committee staff to present client issues and discuss appropriations priorities.

Public Affairs Specialist   2008-2013
Corporation, Inc.   Hours per week: 60

Provides a range of written and verbal information to the media and public. Manages administrative duties and the editorial calendar. Develops outreach programs. In absence of the Public Affairs Director, serve as organizational spokesperson.

- Develop and disseminate information through interviews, press releases, newsletters, customer notices, web postings, email-based customer announcements, and social media.
- Prepare letters, articles, radio and video scripts, talking points, fact sheets, and other materials for use by senior management and news media.
- Interpret information from different departments, then translate it into effective communications for various stakeholders in appropriate formats.
- Responded to hundreds of public information requests via the telephone, Internet, and in writing.
- Consistently maintained historical archive of various District activities and services, including updating chronology, and producing brochures and other related informational historic material.
- Actively identified target audiences for specific outreach efforts, including cross-promotional events and partnerships.

EDUCATION

Bachelor's Degree – 12/2008
Major: Communications
University of Montana

At the end of each checkpoint, we will check in on Susan's progress. Specifically, the **Roadmap to Federal Jobs Worksheet** will guide you (or your client) through following the main steps in this book, making it very easy to map your progress and stay organized.

We will use the worksheet found on the next page to chart Susan's journey to a federal job, and to help you to imagine and formulate your own path.

CareerPro Global
YOUR CAREER IS OUR BUSINESS®

Roadmap to Federal Jobs Worksheet

Instructions: This worksheet is designed to use each time you apply for a federal job. It's best to follow the checkpoints in order, and don't move on until you complete all the steps in a given checkpoint. Once you apply for a job and begin preparing for the interview, simply go back to checkpoint 1 and start again with your next application. Cast a wide net and follow the best practices in the book, and you should eventually find the perfect federal job for you! And remember, you can always refer back to the Roadmap to Federal Jobs book for more detailed information in each area.

(1) Select a Starting Point

List Federal Agencies and Jobs of Interest:

_____

_____

_____

_____

(3) Develop your Federal Resume

Did you identify keywords/headlines/themes?   Y   N

Did you integrate those into your resume?   Y   N

Did you optimize the Additional Information section?
Y   N

Did you edit your resume and check character counts?
Y   N

(2) Determine Your Qualifications for a Specific Job

Write the Job Title/Agency _____

Did you review the duties?   Y   N

Will you be able to show your experience/abilities in your resume?   Y   N

Did you review the special qualifications and/or KSAs?   Y   N

Will you be able to demonstrate your experience in these areas?   Y   N

(4) Develop Knowledge, Skills and Abilities (KSA) Statements

Does the job require KSA essays or mini-KSAs?   Y   N

Did you write them?   Y   N

(5) & (6) Apply for the Job, Follow Up, and Interview Prep

Did you read the job again from top to bottom?   Y   N

Did you review the closing date, how to apply, and required documents?   Y   N

Did you Post Your Resume on USAJOBS.gov?   Y   N

Did you complete the Occupational Questionnaire?   Y   N

Write the date you applied & the job title and #

_____

_____

_____

Did you receive written and/or verbal confirmation?   Y   N

Have you prepared for the interview?   Y   N

Did you follow up after two, four, and/or eight weeks? Y   N

Write down dates of follow up: _____

_____

Checkpoint Notes

Checkpoint 1

Select a Starting Point/Target Job

SELECT A STARTING POINT/TARGET JOB

GETTING STARTED

Many professionals have a range of backgrounds and skills, and, in theory, could thrive in multiple jobs or business areas. But to enter the federal government, you must pick a starting point and then focus your efforts on that job, or type of job. Once you are a federal employee, you can learn more about the working environment and seek promotions and other opportunities as you gain more experience.

Research and Identify Federal Occupation(s) or Agencies of Interest

The first step is to familiarize yourself with the occupational areas in the federal government, and start to zoom in on where you could best serve. The General Schedule (GS) series consists of 23 occupational families that are further divided into more than 400 white-collar occupations. The following are the core GS descriptions; you can find more details online by searching for "OPM general schedule classification qualifications."

GS-000: Miscellaneous

This group includes all classes of positions, the duties of which are to administer, supervise, or perform work that can't be included in other occupational groups.

0006 Correctional Institution Administration Series
0007 Correctional Officer Series
0017 Explosives Safety Series
0018 Safety & Occupational Health Management Series
0019 Safety Technician Series
0020 Community Planning Series
0023 Outdoor Recreation Planning Series
0025 Park Ranger Series
0028 Environmental Protection Specialist Series
0060 Chaplain Series

0062 Clothing Design Series
0072 Fingerprint Identification Series
0080 Security Administration Series
0081 Fire Protection and Prevention Series
0082 United States Marshal Series
0083 Police Series - Grade Evaluation Guide for Police and Security Guard Positions
0084 Nuclear Materials Courier Series
0085 Security Guard Series
0086 Security Clerical and Assistance Series
0090 Guide Series
0095 Foreign Law Specialist Series

GS-100: Social Science, Psychology, and Welfare Group

This group includes all classes of positions, the duties of which are to advise on, administer, supervise, or perform research or other professional and scientific work, subordinate technical work, or related clerical work in one or more of the social sciences: in psychology, in social work, in recreational activities, or in the administration of public welfare and insurance programs.

GS-200: Human Resources Management

This group includes all classes of positions, the duties of which are to advise on, administer, supervise, or perform work involved in the various phases of personnel management.

GS-300: General Administrative, Clerical, and Office Services Group

This group includes all classes of positions, the duties of which are to administer, supervise, or perform work involved in management analysis; stenography, typing, correspondence, and secretarial work; mail and file work; the operation of office appliances; the operation of communications equipment, use of codes and ciphers, and procurement of the most efficient communications services; the operation of microfilm equipment, peripheral equipment, duplicating equipment, mail-processing equipment, and copier/duplicating equipment; and other work of a general clerical and administrative nature.

GS-400: Natural Resources Management and Biological Sciences Group

This group includes all classes of positions, the duties of which are to advise on, administer, supervise, or perform research or other professional and scientific work or subordinate technical work in any of the fields of science concerned with living organisms, their distribution, characteristics, life processes, and adaptations and relations to the environment; the soil, its properties and distribution, and the living organisms growing in or on the soil; and the management, conservation, or utilization thereof for particular purposes or uses.

GS-500: Accounting and Budget Group

This group includes all classes of positions, the duties of which are to advise on, administer, supervise, or perform professional, technical, or related clerical work of an accounting, budget administration, related financial management, or similar nature.

GS-600: Medical, Hospital, Dental, and Public Health Group

This group includes all classes of positions, the duties of

which are to advise on, administer, supervise, or perform research or other professional and scientific work, subordinate technical work, or related clerical work in the several branches of medicine, surgery, and dentistry or in related patient care services, such as dietetics, nursing, occupational therapy, physical therapy, pharmacy, and others.

GS-700: Veterinary Medical Science Group

This group includes all classes of positions, the duties of which are to advise and consult on, administer, manage, supervise, or perform research or other professional and scientific work in the various branches of veterinary medical science.

GS-800: Engineering and Architecture

This group includes all classes of positions, the duties of which are to advise on, administer, supervise, or perform professional, scientific, or technical work concerned with engineering or architectural projects, facilities, structures, systems, processes, equipment, devices, materials, or methods. Positions in this group require knowledge of the science or art—or both—by which materials, natural resources, and power are made useful.

GS-900: Legal and Kindred Group

This group includes all classes of positions, the duties of which are to advise on, administer, supervise, or perform professional legal work in the preparation for trial and the trial and argument of cases; the presiding at formal hearings afforded by a commission, board, or other body having quasi-judicial powers, as part of its administrative procedure; the administration of law entrusted to an agency; the preparation or rendering of authoritative or advisory legal opinions or decisions to other federal agencies or to administrative officials of own agency; the preparation of various legal documents; and the performance of other work requiring training equivalent to that represented by graduation from a recognized law school and, in some instances, requiring admission to the bar; or quasi-legal work that requires knowledge of particular laws, or of regulations, precedents, or departmental practice based thereon, but that does not require such legal training or admission to the bar.

GS-1000: Information and Arts Group

This group includes positions that involve professional, artistic, technical, or clerical work in (1) the communication of information and ideas through verbal, visual, or pictorial means; (2) the collection, custody, presentation, display, and interpretation of art works, cultural objects, and other artifacts; or (3) a branch of fine or applied arts, such as industrial design, interior design, or musical composition.

Positions in this group require writing, editing, and language ability; artistic skill and ability; knowledge of foreign languages; the ability to evaluate and interpret informational and cultural materials; the practical

application of technical or aesthetic principles combined with manual skill; and dexterity and related clerical skills.

GS-1100: Business and Industry Group

This group includes all classes of positions, the duties of which are to advise on, administer, supervise, or perform work pertaining to and requiring a knowledge of business and trade practices, characteristics, and use of equipment, products, or property, or industrial production methods and processes, including the conduct of investigations and studies; the collection, analysis, and dissemination of information; the establishment and maintenance of contracts with industry and commerce; the provision of advisory services; the examination and appraisement of merchandise or property; and the administration of regulatory provisions and controls.

GS-1200: Copyright, Patent, and Trademark Group

This group includes all classes of positions, the duties of which are to advise on, administer, supervise, or perform professional scientific, technical, and legal work involved in the cataloging and registration of copyright, in the classification and issuance of patents, in the registration of trademarks, in the prosecution of applications for patents before the Patent Office, and in the giving of advice to government officials on patent matters.

GS-1300: Physical Science Group

This group includes all classes of positions, the duties of which are to advise on, administer, supervise, or perform research or other professional and scientific work or subordinate technical work in any of the fields of science concerned with matter, energy, physical space, time, nature of physical measurement, and fundamental structural particles, as well as the nature of the physical environment.

GS-1400: Library and Archives Group

This group includes all classes of positions, the duties of which are to advise on, administer, supervise, or perform professional and scientific work or subordinate technical work in the various phases of library archival science.

GS-1500: Mathematics and Statistics Group

This group includes all classes of positions, the duties of which are to advise on, administer, supervise, or perform research or other professional and scientific work or related clerical work in basic mathematical principles, methods, procedures, or relationships, including the development and application of mathematical methods for the investigation and solution of problems; the development and application of statistical theory in the selection, collection, classification, adjustment, analysis, and interpretation of data; the development and application of mathematical, statistical, and financial principles to programs or problems involving life and property risks; and any other professional and scientific or related clerical work requiring primarily and mainly the understanding and use of mathematical theories, methods, and operations.

GS-1600: Equipment, Facilities, and Services Group

This group includes positions, the duties of which are to advise on, manage, or provide instructions and information concerning the operation, maintenance, and use of equipment, shops, buildings, laundries, printing plants, powerplants, cemeteries, or other government facilities, or other work involving services provided predominantly by people in trades, crafts, or manual labor operations. Positions in this group require technical or managerial knowledge and ability in addition to a practical knowledge of trades, crafts, or manual labor operations.

GS-1700: Education Group

This group includes positions that involve administering, managing, supervising, performing, or supporting education or training work when the paramount requirement of the position is knowledge of, or skill in, education, training, or instruction processes.

GS-1800: Inspection, Investigation, Enforcement, and Compliance Group

This group includes all classes of positions, the duties of which are to advise on, administer, supervise, or perform investigation, inspection, or enforcement work primarily concerned with alleged or suspected offenses against the laws of the U.S., or such work primarily concerned with determining compliance with laws and regulations.

GS-1900: Quality Assurance (QA), Inspection, and Grading Group

This group includes all classes of positions, the duties of which are to advise on, supervise, or perform administrative or technical work primarily concerned with the QA or inspection of material, facilities, and processes, or with the grading of commodities under official standards.

GS-2000: Supply Group

This group includes positions that involve work concerned with finishing all types of supplies, equipment, material, property (except real estate), and certain services to components of the federal government, industrial, or other concerns under contract to the government, or receiving supplies from the federal government. Included are positions concerned with one or more aspects of supply activities from initial planning—including requirements analysis and determination—through acquisition, cataloging, storage, distribution, and utilization to ultimate issue for consumption or disposal.

The work requires knowledge of one or more elements or parts of a supply system and/or supply methods, policies, or procedures.

GS-2100: Transportation Group

This group includes all classes of positions, the duties of which are to advise on, administer, supervise, or perform work that involves two or more specialized transportation functions or other transportation work not specifically included in other series of this group.

GS-2200: Information Technology (IT) Group

This group includes all positions for the administrative work in IT. The primary subcategory is 2210, which covers IT management. Within IT management are 11 possible areas of responsibility (or combination of responsibilities).

Wage Grade Trades and Labor Job Families and Occupations

The Wage Grade (WG) group offers an additional 36 occupational families: WG-2500 through WG-9000. These are typically considered the blue-collar positions. The following is a list of the WG family groups; you can find more information by searching for "OPM WG classification standards."

- WG-2500 Wire Communications Equipment Installation/Maintenance
- WG-2600 Equipment Installation and Maintenance
- WG-2800 Electrical Installation and Maintenance
- WG-3100 Fabric and Leather Work
- WG-3300 Instrument Work
- WG-3400 Machine Tool Work
- WG-3500 General Services and Support Work
- WG-3600 Structural and Finishing Work
- WG-3700 Metal Processing
- WG-3800 Metal Working
- WG-3900 Motion Picture, Radio, TV, and Sound Equipment Operation

> **Take Note**
>
> The best way to distinguish between the General Schedule (GS) and Wage Grade group (WG) occupations is to think of the distinction in terms of professional and trade jobs that are commonly found in the private sector.
>
> The GS positions are typically the white-collar (office) jobs that are considered non-exempt (meaning they generally don't have overtime for any hours worked beyond a standard 40-hour workweek.)
>
> WG occupations are typically the same as the blue-collar or hourly positions, and most of these jobs require some sort of specialized training or knowledge.

- WG-4000 Lens and Crystal Work
- WG-4100 Painting and Paperhanging
- WG-4200 Plumbing and Pipe fitting
- WG-4300 Pliable Materials Work
- WG-4400 Printing
- WG-4600 Woodwork
- WG-4700 General Maintenance and Operations Work
- WG-4800 General Equipment Maintenance
- WG-5000 Plant and Animal Work
- WG-5200 Miscellaneous Occupations
- WG-5300 Industrial Equipment Maintenance
- WG-5400 Industrial Equipment Operation
- WG-5700 Transportation/Mobile Equipment Operation
- WG-5800 Heavy Mobile Equipment Mechanic
- WG-6500 Ammunition, Explosives, and Toxic Materials Work
- WG-6600 Armament Work
- WG-6900 Warehousing and Stock Handling
- WG-7000 Packing and Processing
- WG-7300 Laundry, Dry Cleaning, and Pressing
- WG-7400 Food Preparation and Servicing
- WG-7600 Personal Services
- WG-8200 Fluid Systems Maintenance
- WG-8600 Engine Overhaul

- WG-8800 Aircraft Overhaul
- WG-9000 Film Processing

Next, you want to focus even more and research agencies or programs you would like to join. You can research all the government's agencies easily online, and by using this link: USA.gov/federal-agencies. After reviewing an agency's history, mission, and other materials, you may come closer to a decision.

Pick a Job or Occupational Series

The next step is to select an actual vacancy within that agency, or at least the occupational series you choose. This is done through USAJOBS.gov, the federal government's official employment website.

If you can find positions of interest in the specific agency you want, then great! But quite often, people like to simply search USAJOBS.gov using keywords or occupational series to see what's available across the government. In addition to allowing you to search and apply for jobs, USAJOBS.gov will let you:

- Determine applicable pay scale. If the position begins with GS, you should refer to the General Schedule; if it's WG, it's the Wage Grade.

- Build and store up to five unique resumes in your personal and secure online account area. Applicants may also upload up to two resumes to USAJOBS. These resumes can be released to various jobs for which candidates have determined they are a match.

- Set up and save automatic job searches. Applicants should put USAJOBS to work by setting up an automatic job search agent that will scan the various vacancies every day and email you when openings that match your criteria become available. This is a great way to be proactive and maximize the time you have left to work on your application materials (resume,

questionnaires, etc.).

- Manage your various applications. USAJOBS.gov and its sister site, Application Manager (http://www.applicationmanager.gov), will provide updated information regarding the status of submitted applications.

Searching for a Job on USAJOBS.gov

The USAJOBS.gov website has undergone many updates and changes over the years, and is now more functional and user-friendly than ever. For instance, in 2016 and 2017, the site launched several new features, including:

- The entire online application process was updated.

- The USAJOBS Help Center and "Contact Us" page has been revamped and now lists agency recruiting events and job fairs.

- They added a profile dashboard that lets you easily view the status of your applications and review saved job announcements and searches.

- They added new search technology to deliver faster and more relevant job search results.

- You now have the ability to search for jobs based on unique hiring paths. They added hiring path filters to the search feature to increase their visibility and help you find jobs based on your eligibility. You can see all the hiring paths on the USAJOBS.gov homepage, and learn more about eligibility here: https://www.usajobs.gov/Help/faq/application/eligibility/

- You can now search for positions based on country, state, and zip code, and filter search results based on a variety of criteria, such as pay, work schedule, security clearance level requirements, department, and appointment type.

- Job searches are now more intuitive because the basic and advanced search options have been combined into one search view, which will yield better and more relevant results. These new filter options basically replace the old "advanced search" feature. The site also offers lots of helpful tutorials and information here: https://www.usajobs.gov/Help/

At the end of the day, you simply want to use agency names, occupational series, or relevant keywords to begin your search and narrow down your options.

Creating Saved Searches

Candidates seeking federal employment can take advantage of the search agent function on USAJOBS.gov. Applicants can establish searches by geographic location, grade, pay, job category, and/or agency. This way, you'll be the first to know when a suitable vacancy becomes available, and can avoid the last-minute rush to put together a federal resume application package.

The website has many useful instructions at this link: https://www.usajobs.gov/Help/how-to/search/save/.

Here Are the Steps Provided to Create a Saved Search and Sign Up for Email Notifications:

1. Sign into your USAJOBS account. If you don't have an account, you need to create one. Only signed-in users can save their search.

2. Start a job search by entering a keyword or location in the search box and click "Search." You can also choose the Advanced Search option to narrow your results.

3. Click "Save This Search" on the search results page located on the left side of the page under the search filters.

4. Enter additional search criteria if you want; the more information you add, the more specific your results will be.

5. Name your search—this will help you manage your saved searches.

6. Choose how often you want to receive an email notification with all jobs that match your search. We recommend daily notifications if you're looking for very specific positions, since some announcements can open and close within a week. If you select daily, you'll receive one email per day only if new jobs have been posted that match your criteria in the last 24 hours.

7. Click "Save Search" or "Save and View Results." By clicking the latter, you can see if the saved search returns the results you want. If not, you can edit the saved search.

Susan's Story and Worksheet

By this point, you should have a good idea of which occupational series, agencies, and specific jobs interest you, and you should know how to search for them on USAJOBS.gov.

Let's check in on Susan, who is leaning toward using her skills as a Public Affairs Specialist (1035 Occupational Series) or Legislative Affairs Specialist (0301 Miscellaneous Administration and Program Series).

On the next page, you can see what Susan's worksheet would look like so far.

CareerPro Global
YOUR CAREER IS OUR BUSINESS®

Roadmap to Federal Jobs Worksheet

Instructions: This worksheet is designed to use each time you apply for a federal job. It's best to follow the checkpoints in order, and don't move on until you complete all the steps in a given checkpoint. Once you apply for a job and begin preparing for the interview, simply go back to checkpoint 1 and start again with your next application. Cast a wide net and follow the best practices in the book, and you should eventually find the perfect federal job for you! And remember, you can always refer back to the Roadmap to Federal Jobs book for more detailed information in each area.

① Select a Starting Point

List Federal Agencies and Jobs of Interest:

Department of Homeland Security

U.S. Agency for International Development

Legislative Affairs

Public Affairs

② Determine Your Qualifications for a Specific Job

Write the Job Title/Agency _____

Did you review the duties?   Y   N

Will you be able to show your experience/abilities in your resume?   Y   N

Did you review the special qualifications and/or KSAs?   Y   N

Will you be able to demonstrate your experience in these areas?   Y   N

③ Develop your Federal Resume

Did you identify keywords/headlines/themes?   Y   N

Did you integrate those into your resume?   Y   N

Did you optimize the Additional Information section?   Y   N

Did you edit your resume and check character counts?   Y   N

④ Develop Knowledge, Skills and Abilities (KSA) Statements

Does the job require KSA essays or mini-KSAs?   Y   N

Did you write them?   Y   N

⑤ & ⑥ Apply for the Job, Follow Up, and Interview Prep

Did you read the job again from top to bottom?   Y   N

Did you review the closing date, how to apply, and required documents?   Y   N

Did you Post Your Resume on USAJOBS.gov?   Y   N

Did you complete the Occupational Questionnaire?   Y   N

Write the date you applied & the job title and #

_____

_____

Did you receive written and/or verbal confirmation?   Y   N

Have you prepared for the interview?   Y   N

Did you follow up after two, four, and/or eight weeks? Y   N

Write down dates of follow up: _____

_____

CareerPro Global, Inc. | (800) 471-9201 | www.careerproplus.com | www.militaryresumewriters.com

Checkpoint Notes

Checkpoint Notes

Checkpoint 2

Determine Your Qualifications for a Specific Job

DETERMINE YOUR QUALIFICATIONS FOR A SPECIFIC JOB

WHAT'S IMPORTANT ABOUT FEDERAL JOB ANNOUNCEMENTS?

Often, someone exploring federal employment for the first time will focus on job description, salary, and location—basically, the items that they're looking for in a job. However, many don't examine their eligibility and qualifications for the position, nor do they follow the application instructions. Thus, they are not referred to the position, regardless of how qualified they may be.

Although the Office of Personnel Management (OPM) has standardized the format used for federal vacancy announcements, it's important to remember that not every announcement is created equally. For example, some announcements are more detailed, while others are quite sparse on information. Further, vacancy announcements for those Excepted Service/direct hire positions may look quite different. Whatever the case, if you understand the different parts of an announcement, you'll be able to confidently navigate the federal application process.

The Anatomy of a Federal Vacancy Announcement

Vacancy Announcement Number: This is the identification number issued to each vacancy announcement. Be sure to reference this number on all application materials.

Opening Date: This is the date when the vacancy announcement was initially opened for submission of applications.

Closing Date: This is the final date that applications may be submitted for consideration for an available position. Applicants should read this carefully; many announcements close at 11:59 p.m. EST while others may close at other times. Deadlines are rarely extended, so it's your responsibility to get your application in by the closing date. We recommend submitting your application at least one business day before the job closes, so that you can call in, if there are any issues.

Position: This is the title of the vacancy being announced.

Series and Grade: This information indicates the pay plan, series, and grade for the available position. Some positions are posted at multiple grades, so apply for every grade you are willing to accept, and do not assume that the agency will automatically consider you for every grade available.

Promotion Potential: This information will indicate whether the available position has the potential for promotion as well as describe the full performance level. Generally, positions filled at a grade lower than the full performance level have non-competitive promotion potential to the full performance level. This means that employees will not have to compete again to reach the position's full performance level.

Salary: This is the salary range for the available position.

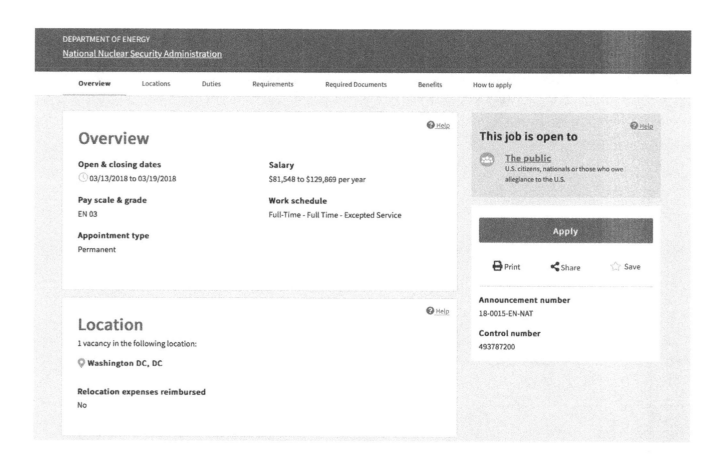

DEPARTMENT OF ENERGY
National Nuclear Security Administration

Overview   Locations   Duties   Requirements   Required Documents   Benefits   How to apply

Overview   ❓ Help

Open & closing dates   **Salary**
🕐 03/13/2018 to 03/19/2018 $81,548 to $129,869 per year

Pay scale & grade   **Work schedule**
EN 03   Full-Time - Full Time - Excepted Service

Appointment type
Permanent

This job is open to   ❓ Help

😀 The public
    U.S. citizens, nationals or those who owe
    allegiance to the U.S.

        Apply

🖨 Print   ◀ Share   ☆ Save

Announcement number
18-0015-EN-NAT

Control number
493787200

Location   ❓ Help
1 vacancy in the following location:

📍 Washington DC, DC

Relocation expenses reimbursed
No

Duty Location: This is the geographic location where the position will be filled, or where the position is located.

Who May Apply: This area describes who is eligible to apply for the available position, such as "Federal Civil Service Employees" or "Public."

When a vacancy announcement states that it's open for Merit Promotion (MP), this means that applications will be accepted from current Competitive Service federal employees, Veterans Employment Opportunity Act (VEOA) eligibles (those with three or more years of Active Duty military service) or employees who are reinstatement eligible (held a Competitive Service position in the past).

Working for a federal contractor or being a former military service member does not constitute "federal

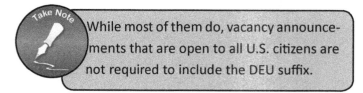

While most of them do, vacancy announcements that are open to all U.S. citizens are not required to include the DEU suffix.

employment status." When the vacancy number includes the suffix "DEU," for Delegated Examining Unit, this means that applications will be accepted from all U.S. citizens.

Major Duties: This is where they tell you exactly what the job entails, so it's important to ask yourself honestly if you can perform those duties. Most importantly, consider if you will be able to "prove," or demonstrate in your resume, that you have the experience, training, and knowledge to perform those duties?

Qualifications Required: These are the basic qualification levels on which an applicant will be considered, and sometimes they present these as Knowledge, Skills, and Abilities (KSAs), core competencies, or specialized experience. For example, if a candidate is a GS-7 Clerk, that means h/she is not automatically eligible for a GS-7 Budget Analyst position.

Applicants are required to have one year of specialized experience in order to meet the eligibility requirements of the GS-7 Budget Analyst to be ranked as eligible. A good rule of thumb is that if you don't possess the specialized experience requirements, you're not well qualified for the position and will not be a strong candidate.

Duties

Summary

A successful candidate in this position will serve as a Program Analyst, Legislative Matters & Records, performs NNSA planning, advocacy, and execution duties, providing essential information for Congressional inspection, review and decision making.

> Learn more about this agency

Responsibilities

As a Program Analyst, you will:

- Serve as the focal point for contacts between the NNSA and OMB regarding testimony on program and budget matters.
- Exercise considerable tact and diplomacy in the management of the notification process in order to maintain proper protocol and to effectively serve the best interests of the National Nuclear Security Administration (NNSA).
- Recommed procedures and policies governing interaction between National Nuclear Security Administration (NNSA) offices, other government agencies, OMB, and the Congress in order to ensure the effective coordination of legislative hearings for the National Nuclear Security Administration (NNSA).
- Keep officials informed on testimony, staff responses to Q & A's, on coordination activities with OMB having an impact on the mission and objectives of the Administration as they relate to Congress.

Travel Required

Occasional travel - This position requires travel outside of the duty station 10% of the time.

With this in mind, be sure your resume provides information that clearly demonstrates that you meet the specialized experience requirements or any core competencies.

How You Will Be Evaluated: This section describes how applicants will be evaluated for the position—whether they will be ranked on their KSAs or other characteristics required to perform the duties of the position. You should also review this information, including any questionnaires, very carefully.

Some jobs have an educational requirement, so this

should be a critical part of your review process. If you can't provide one or two strong examples of demonstrating each KSA and/or give the best possible answer to the questions on the questionnaire, then the sought-after position may not be the best match at this time.

How You Will Be Evaluated

You will be evaluated for this job based on how well you meet the qualifications above.

Your application will be rated by our application system using the Category Rating procedure. A quality review will then be conducted by the HR Office and/or Subject Matter Expert (SME). Your application is rated based on the extent and quality of your experience, education (if applicable to the job), and training described in your online resume/questionnaire as related to the duties of this position. The quality categories are usually defined as "Best Qualified", "Well Qualified" and "Qualified". Veterans Preference eligible will be listed at the top of whichever category your score places you in. CP/CPS veterans are placed at the top of the highest category for all positions except professional and scientific positions at GS-9 and higher.

Your performance appraisals and incentive awards will be given due consideration in the selection process based on their relation to the duties of the position and the consistency with which they may be considered in evaluating you against other applicants.

If you are eligible for career transition assistance plans such as ICTAP or CTAP, you must meet the definition of "well qualified" which is defined as having a score of 85 or better.

If your resume is incomplete or does not support the responses you provided in your online questionnaire, or if you fail to submit all required documentation before the vacancy closes, you may be rated 'ineligible', 'not qualified', or your score may be adjusted accordingly.

To preview questions please <u>click here</u>.

What Is Most Important?

As you can see, there's a lot of information in a typical job announcement, and we always recommend reading the announcement from top to bottom—several times.

When you're trying to decide if a job is a good fit for your background and experience, it's important to focus on the closing date, the job duties, any special qualifications, educational requirements, KSAs, and the occupational questionnaire.

More About Specialized Qualifications

Here is an example of the qualification requirements for a Supervisory Staff Accountant, GS-0510-13/14. This particular position lists the Basic Qualifications (Education and Experience); it also lists a **SPECIALIZED EXPERIENCE** condition that must be met.

To meet the specialized experience for this position, you must meet the following definitions, relative to the grade(s) for which you are applying:

<u>**GS-13:**</u> You must possess one year of specialized experience equivalent to the GS-12 level in the Federal Service. Such experience is defined as: reviewing, analyzing, and validating institutional financial data and resolving accounting discrepancies sufficient to support the administrative operations of an organization charged with the administration and accounting of federal funds.

<u>**GS-14:**</u> You must possess one year of specialized experience equivalent to the GS-13 level in the Federal Service. Such experience is defined as: experience applying accounting, finance, and grants management practices to provide expert support to the administrative operations of an organization charged with the administration and accounting of federal funds.

Sometimes an announcement will list what's known as a **SELECTIVE PLACEMENT FACTOR** or **SCREEN-OUT ELEMENT**. Simply put, these are specialized requirements and core competencies that you must meet. If not, the hiring authority will deem you ineligible, and no further consideration will be granted.

The following is a Screen-Out Element for an Air Conditioning Equipment Mechanic, WG-5306-08. Note the emphasis placed on the underlined text as something you would have to pay close attention to and demonstrate in the resume:

Applicants must meet the Screen-Out Element, <u>which is the ability to do the work of an Air Conditioning Equipment Mechanic without more-than-normal supervision.</u> If you don't meet the Screen-Out Element, you will be evaluated as "ineligible." Applicants must also possess the following job elements: <u>Able to assemble, make, install, test, and repair a variety of domestic, industrial, and commercial systems.</u>

<u>Ability to do the theoretical, precise, and/or artistic work of an Air Conditioning Equipment Mechanic. Ability to interpret instructions, specifications, and blueprints. Ability to use and maintain tools, instruments, and related equipment, as appropriate. Knowledge of all materials used</u> within the trade. Ability to find, troubleshoot, and determine method of repair and use appropriate tests.

Selective Placement Factors are also used for GS positions. Here is an example of Watch Officer, GS-343-11/12 at the Federal Emergency Management Agency (FEMA):

QUALIFICATIONS REQUIRED:
Specialized Experience Requirements: <u>Applicants must have one year of specialized experience equivalent to the next lower grade level in the Federal Service.</u> Specialized experience is experience that equipped the applicant with the knowledge, skills, and abilities to perform successfully the duties of the position and that is in, or related to, the work of the position to be filled.

Specialized experience is described as <u>experience in ap-</u>

<u>plying the concepts, theories, principles, and practices of emergency management to collect and analyze data from a variety of sources in order to develop specialized reports, summaries, and briefings used to mitigate risks. This experience could have been gained by working in a 24/7 operations center.</u>

Selective Placement Factor: <u>At least one year of experience as a Watch Officer/Analyst in a Command or watch center at the federal, state, or local level.</u> Applicants without the SPF will not be considered further.

As a general rule, demonstrated experience is preferred by hiring officials and can earn a candidate the "Best Qualified" rating. It should be noted here that some positions, such as a Contracting Specialist or an Accountant, have education requirements in addition to experience. Applicants without the required education will not be considered, no matter how much experience they have.

However, if an announcement does allow for education, the following guidelines will help you determine what grade level will be the best fit. The table on the next page provides an overview of what is generally required, at minimum, to qualify for a grade.

Common Federal Vacancy Terminology
You might encounter the following additional terms when reviewing vacancy announcements:

Career and Career-Conditional Employee: Permanent federal career status is automatically gained upon completion of the mandatory three-year career-

GRADE	QUALIFYING EDUCATION
GS-1	None
GS-2	High-school graduation or equivalent
GS-3	1 academic year above high school
GS-4	2 academic years above high school, **OR** Associate's degree
GS-5	4 academic years above high school leading to a Bachelor's degree; **OR** Bachelor's degree
GS-7	Bachelor's degree with Superior Academic Achievement for two-grade interval positions, **OR** 1 academic year of graduate education (or law school, as specified in qualification standards or individual occupational requirements)
GS-9	Master's (or equivalent graduate degree such as LL.B. or J.D. as specified in qualification standards or individual occupational requirements), **OR** 2 academic years of progressively higher-level graduate education
GS-11	Ph.D. or equivalent doctoral degree, **OR** 3 academic years of progressively higher-level graduate education, **OR** for research positions only, completion of all requirements for a Master's or equivalent degree
GS-12	For research positions only, completion of all requirements for a doctoral or equivalent degree.

conditional period. These candidates are also known as "status candidates."

Creditable Service: This refers to federal government employment (civilian or uniformed service) that meets requirements for a particular type of appointment or benefit, such as leave accrual or Reduction in Force (RIF) retention.

Declaration for Federal Employment: This form documents a candidate's fulfillment of the two requirements for federal employment: U.S. citizenship and, for men born after December 31, 1959, compliance with U.S. Selective Service registration.

Knowledge, Skills, and Abilities (KSAs): This defines the fundamental knowledge, skills, and abilities required for the particular position. These may also be presented as core competencies.

Occupational Questionnaire: These questions, usually posted online, typically consist of a combination of multiple choice, yes/no, and short narratives, which are designed to further assess your qualifications. Some questionnaires also require the completion of narratives to substantiate multiple-choice answers. Regardless of whether the questionnaire requires narrative responses, all claims made in the questionnaire should be documented in your resume in order to receive full credit.

OPM (Office of Personnel Management): The government's main HR agency.

Veterans' Preference: This refers to an employee's category of entitlement preference in the Federal Service based on active military service that was terminated honorably and that meets specific criteria.

Qualifications Standards Operating Manual: This is the published guide to qualifications required for GS positions in the federal government. It outlines minimum experience and/or education requirements for each job series.

Status Candidates: These are job applicants who currently work for the federal government or certain former federal employees who held (or hold) Competitive Service positions.

Temporary: As the name suggests, temporary positions are filled for one year or less; employees chosen for these jobs do not receive benefits.

Term Position: A term position is a non-permanent position that can last anywhere from one to four years. Employees who fill term positions generally receive the same benefits as permanent employees, but don't have status.

Superior Qualifications Appointment: This refers to placement of a person in a hard-to-recruit-for position at a pay rate above the minimum Step 1 for a particular grade, based on the applicant's unique or unusually high qualifications, a special government need for applicants' services, and/or the fact that applicants' present salary or salary offerings are higher than the minimum rate of the grade level to which the applicant can be appointed. This is negotiated individually between the successful applicant and the agency and is not guaranteed.

How to Apply: Here you will find specific instructions for applying, and if you have questions, don't be shy! Email the contact person on the job so that you have a paper trail and official record of their response. You can also call in with any questions.

Required Documents: This section of the job announcement will tell you exactly what they want, and will sometimes include formatting instructions for your documents. You want to submit exactly what they

How to Apply

To be considered for this position, you must submit your complete application no later than 11:59pm U.S. Eastern Time on the closing date of this announcement. If you do not submit a complete application prior to the closing time (regardless of when you started) the online application system will not allow you to finish! Requests for extensions will not be granted, so please begin the application process allowing yourself enough time to finish before the deadline. Our online application system displays a countdown timer at the top of the screen for your reference.

For your security, your session in our online application system will "time-out" if you are inactive for a certain period of time. We recommend that you preview the assessment questions before you apply and prepare all of your information prior to beginning the application. If you do get "timed-out" you will have to log back in to USAJOBS and re-visit the vacancy announcement, you can then click "Update Application" to finish where you left off.

Steps to submit a complete application:

1. Click the "Apply Online" button. If you are not already logged in, you will need to do so.

2. You must have a complete resume associated with your USAJOBS account. *Please note that some DOE offices do not accept uploaded resumes and instead require that you submit a USAJOBS-formatted resume using the Resume Builder.*

3. You will be prompted to select a resume and any documentation you have attached to your USAJOBS account before you are transferred to the Department of Energy's online application system. Please be aware that any document you select before being transferred to our system, will not automatically be received. You must take steps to download your documents from USAJOBS during the "Documents" step within our online application system (see Step 6).

4. If you are a first-time applicant to the Department of Energy, you'll be asked to register an account first. If you are a returning applicant, you will skip this step and go straight to the application portion.

5. You must respond to all applicant assessment questions, carefully following all instructions provided.

6. You will then be asked to upload additional supporting documentation. If you selected documents from USAJOBS prior to being transferred to our application system (Step 3), you will need to click the "USAJOBS" link to complete the transfer process. These documents ARE NOT automatically transferred! *It is ultimately your responsibility to make sure all required documents are either faxed, uploaded, or transferred from USAJOBS successfully. If you are unsure that your documents went through, please contact the HR Specialist listed on the announcement BEFORE the vacancy closes.*

7. After reviewing your submission in the final step, you must click "Submit Application" at the bottom of the page. If you leave the application before clicking Submit, your application will not be received.

If your resume does not support the responses in your application questionnaire, or if you fail to submit required documentation before the vacancy closes, you may be rated 'ineligible', 'not qualified', or your score may be adjusted accordingly.

ask for—nothing more and nothing less. If you have any questions, email the HR contact person.

"PRE-QUALIFY" YOURSELF TO SAVE TIME

By reviewing the important spots highlighted above, you can "pre-qualify" yourself. This saves time, because if there is an educational, time-in-grade, or other requirement that you lack, you may decide not to apply.

But then again, what if you meet all the qualifications, but the duties seem like a professional "stretch," or you have similar experience, but not exactly the way it's listed?

That's okay; go for it! Just do your best to demonstrate your related experience and potential throughout your resume.

Susan's Story and Worksheet

Susan has decided to apply for a GS-11 Legislative Affairs Specialist job in the Department of Homeland Security (DHS). Review the details of the vacancy announcement on the next two pages. After that, we'll see what Susan's worksheet would look like so far.

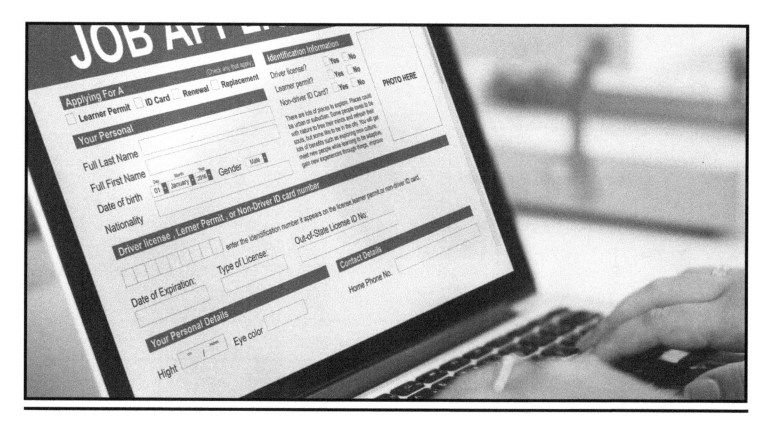

Supervisory Legislative Affairs Specialist

DEPARTMENT OF HOMELAND SECURITY

DHS Headquarters

Office of Legislative Affairs

Overview

Open & closing dates

⊘ 12/04/2017 to 12/08/2017

Salary

$131,767 to $161,900 per year

There is no optional salary for this position; the salary is stated as listed above

Pay scale & grade

GS 15

Work schedule

Full-Time

Appointment type

Permanent

Locations

1 vacancy in the following location:

District of Columbia, DC

Relocation expenses reimbursed

No

This job is open to

The public

U.S. citizens, nationals or those who owe allegiance to the U.S., and excepted service employees.

Duties

Summary

The Department of Homeland Security (DHS) is calling on those who want to help protect American interests and secure our Nation. DHS Components work collectively to prevent terrorism; secure borders and our transportation systems; protect the President and other dignitaries; enforce and administer immigration laws; safeguard cyberspace; and ensure resilience to disasters. We achieve these vital missions through a diverse workforce spanning hundreds of occupations. Make an impact; join DHS.

Any offers of employment made pursuant to this announcement will be consistent with all applicable authorities, including Presidential Memoranda, Executive Orders, Interpretive U. S. Office of Management and Budget (OMB) and U. S. Office of Personnel Management (OPM) guidance, and Office of Management and Budget plans and policies concerning hiring. These authorities are subject to change.

This position is located in the Department of Homeland Security (DHS), Office of the Secretary, Office of Legislative Affairs (OLA). The mission of OLA is to maximize the service of DHS to the American public by establishing and enduring, trusted partnership with the Congress of the United States, by providing Members and staff the timely, accurate, and detailed information needs to fulfill their
constitutional duties by clearly articulating DHS views in support of needed authorities and appropriations; and by working constructively with the Congress to ensure careful stewardship of DHS resources. .

This position starts at a salary of $131,767, GS-15 grade level. This position is at the full performance level

All DHS-HQ announcements have a 5 business day open period due to the number of applications received.

Applying to this announcement certifies that you give permission for DHS to share your application with others in DHS for similar positions.

Responsibilities

As a Supervisory Legislative Affairs Specialist GS 0301 15, your typical work assignments may include:

- Works closely with Assistant Secretary for Legislative Affairs and other offices.
- Possesses a thorough knowledge of the program portfolio such as the emergency management, transportation security, and Grant Programs.
- Provides advice and guidance to Department Senior leadership in the development and establishment of hearing schedules, processes and procedures.
- Exercises supervisory and managerial authority, at least 25% of the time, over legislative affairs specialists.

CareerPro Global
YOUR CAREER IS OUR BUSINESS®

Roadmap to Federal Jobs Worksheet

Instructions: This worksheet is designed to use each time you apply for a federal job. It's best to follow the checkpoints in order, and don't move on until you complete all the steps in a given checkpoint. Once you apply for a job and begin preparing for the interview, simply go back to checkpoint 1 and start again with your next application. Cast a wide net and follow the best practices in the book, and you should eventually find the perfect federal job for you! And remember, you can always refer back to the Roadmap to Federal Jobs book for more detailed information in each area.

① Select a Starting Point

List Federal Agencies and Jobs of Interest:

Department of Homeland Security

U.S. Agency for International Development

Legislative Affairs

Public Affairs

② Determine Your Qualifications for a Specific Job

Write the Job Title/Agency *DHS, Legislative Affairs, Job No. 339-DHS-59917*

Did you review the duties? (Y) N

Will you be able to show your experience/abilities in your resume? (Y) N

Did you review the special qualifications and/or KSAs? (Y) N

Will you be able to demonstrate your experience in these areas? (Y) N

③ Develop your Federal Resume

Did you identify keywords/headlines/themes?   Y   N

Did you integrate those into your resume?   Y   N

Did you optimize the Additional Information section?
Y   N

Did you edit your resume and check character counts?
Y   N

④ Develop Knowledge, Skills and Abilities (KSA) Statements

Does the job require KSA essays or mini-KSAs?   Y   N

Did you write them?   Y   N

⑤ & ⑥ Apply for the Job, Follow Up, and Interview Prep

Did you read the job again from top to bottom?   Y   N

Did you review the closing date, how to apply, and required documents?   Y   N

Did you Post Your Resume on USAJOBS.gov?   Y   N

Did you complete the Occupational Questionnaire?   Y   N

Write the date you applied & the job title and #

_____

_____

_____

Did you receive written and/or verbal confirmation?   Y   N

Have you prepared for the interview?   Y   N

Did you follow up after two, four, and/or eight weeks? Y   N

Write down dates of follow up: _____

_____

CareerPro Global, Inc. | (800) 471-9201 | www.careerproplus.com | www.militaryresumewriters.com

Checkpoint Notes

Checkpoint Notes

Checkpoint 3

Develop an Effective Federal Resume

Check Point 3

DEVELOP AN EFFECTIVE FEDERAL RESUME

ANATOMY OF A FEDERAL RESUME

A strong resume is critical, since it's a requirement for federal positions, and it's is usually the very first thing a hiring manager will see.

If it's put together well, and clearly tells the reader about your relevant background and what you can offer, then you're much more likely to land an interview. If it's boring, poorly designed, or poorly written, it comes off as unprofessional and doesn't motivate the hiring manager to continue reading or consider interviewing you.

First, let's do a brief overview of the different sections in the USAJOBS resume builder, so we can begin to understand how to optimize them for the best possible results.

- **Work Experience**
- **Education:** School Name, 100 characters; Major and Minor, 60 characters each
- **Relevant Coursework, Licensures and Certifications:** 2,000 characters characters/space
- **Job Related Training:** Maximum of 5,000 characters/ spaces
- **Organizations/Affiliations:** Maximum of four listings

- **Publications:** Maximum 5,000 characters characters/ spaces
- **Additional Information:** Maximum of 20,000 characters/spaces

Okay, you've now completed Checkpoint 2. You should have a specific vacancy announcement, a sample vacancy announcement, or at least an occupational series you would like to target.

Documents You Might Need and WHY

VMET (Verification of Military Experience and Training)	Gives you a consolidated view of all your military assignments and training
DD-214 (record of separation)	Gives you dates of service and other basic information
List of Job-Related Skills	Reminds you of what types of positions you want to—and should—target
Letters of Recommendation	Gives you potential quotes and references
Performance Appraisals	Gives you specific accomplishments and possibly some supportive quotes about your performance
College Transcripts	Help you remember specific courses that might be relevant
Training Certificates	Details about what you learned, accomplished/became certified in
Awards Citations and Honors	Shows how you excelled and gives potential quotes about your performance
List of Affiliations	Shows with which organizations you are aligned
List of Publications	Shows that you have been published and possess strong writing skills
List of Speaking Engagements	Shows that you are comfortable and confident speaking in front of people
Official Orders	Can help you remember special assignments/accomplishments

You understand the different sections you'll need to complete in the builder. Now you're ready for the five-step resume development process.

Step 1. Use a Job or Sample Vacancy Announcement to Identify Keywords/Headlines/Core Competencies

To stand out and optimize your resume, any keywords or recurring phrases in the vacancy announcement should be extracted and utilized by connecting your experiences to those core performance expectations. Further, you want to use keywords throughout the resume, but especially in the work history and professional summary.

In most cases, keywords are nouns. What types of nouns are sought? Nouns that relate to the skills and experience the employer is looking for in a candidate are the ones to shoot for.

More specifically, keywords and core competencies can be precise "hard" skills—job-specific/profession-specific/industry-specific skills, technological terms, and descriptions of technical expertise (including hardware and software in which the client is proficient), job titles, certifications, names of products and services, industry buzzwords and jargon, types of degrees, names of colleges, company names, terms that tend to impress, such as "Fortune 500," and even area codes for narrowing down searches geographically.

Where Do You Find Keywords?

Keywords are intentionally placed in all vacancy job announcements. You can find keywords in job vacancy announcements under three sections: Job Summary, Major Duties, and Qualifications (specialized experience and how you will be evaluated). You might also find keywords in:

- Job-description books
- OPM Classification Standards
- OPM Qualification Standards
- Websites of professional associations in your field to look and listen for current buzzwords
- Government publications, such as the "Occupational Outlook Handbook," at libraries or online
- Website of the employer you are targeting; look for keywords describing the organization's culture and values; note the mission statement and look for ways to quote it in your resume
- Web search engines, such as Google and Yahoo, to search for job descriptions

Below is an example from a Senior IT Project Manager vacancy announcement. Note the words and phrases that are underlined.

The Senior IT Project Manager must be able to oversee large, complex projects, control and understand the business environment and work product, and evaluate technical specifications. Key responsibilities include directing and evaluating project vision and strategy, accountability for project completion and team management, defining and driving project deliverables, and facilitating development and operations project teams.

The Senior IT Project Manager is responsible for defining, creating, and maintaining a project plan, managing daily client communication, allocating resources, and maintaining team productivity and morale in high-pressure situations. Candidates must have IT expertise, a Bachelor's degree in management, engineering, computer science, business, or similar field, 4+ years' experience in professional services or consulting, 2+ years of managerial

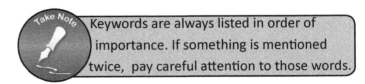 Keywords are always listed in order of importance. If something is mentioned twice, pay careful attention to those words.

experience, and the ability to manage multidisciplinary projects with 10+ people.

Duties/Responsibilities:
- Work with the prospective professional services customer to define the scope of work and provide it to the customer for approval.
- Identify the external resources and, if appropriate, internal resources with the necessary skills to develop a detailed Statement of Work.
- Manage the Professional Services team to execute on and complete the deliverables called out in the Statement of Work.
- Manage the client relationship.

Qualifications:
-Demonstrated management, leadership, communication, motivational, and influencing skills.

-Must have a thorough understanding of the software development process, preferably from a system (hardware/software) perspective.

-Must have a proven record of managing software/hardware system integration projects/programs.

-Must feel comfortable in a leadership role in a matrix management environment

-Must be able to effectively communicate both verbally and in writing with individual contributors, management, executive staff, as well as with the customer.

-Problem-solver with the ability to provide primary problem diagnosis and coordinate resolution.

On the next page is a sample vacancy announcement for a Supervisory Program Manager, GS-0340-14 with keywords highlighted:

DUTIES:

In this position, you will become a key member of law enforcement and fire prevention and protection professionals in a pivotal role from day one. You will aid the Division Director in overseeing the Emergency Services Division and all matters related to emergency preparedness, mitigation, and recovery of MWEOC Emergency Services missions. Typical work assignments include:

- Providing administrative and technical management necessary for Fire, Police, and Security Chiefs to coordinate actual or potential emergency preparedness or response efforts and coordinate training programs and emergency operations and drills to prepare staff to respond quickly and effectively to emergencies.
- Coordinating and directing the accomplishment of emergency planning concepts necessary to develop an integrated, generic, comprehensive emergency operations plan.
- Providing expert analysis and advice on agency-wide programs or issues of national impact.
- Serving as a technical expert, providing professional advice and guidance on operations and services involving emergency services and hazardous materials before, during, and after emergency situations.

Using the Headline Format

CareerPro Global, Inc. developed the Headline Format-Style Resume in 1990 to assist veterans returning from Operations Desert Shield and Desert Storm. By utilizing this resume format, CPG's writing team was able to best describe an area of expertise held by a veteran in terms that civilian employers could understand through the use of **KEYWORDS** and **CORE COMPETENCIES**.

CPG adapted the Headline Format-Style Resume on all federal resume applications in 1995, when the SF-171 was eliminated and regular paper federal resumes and online systems were launched. Today, we use the Headline Format-Style Resume on all federal job applications to draw attention to specific areas of expertise and core competencies to assist federal hiring managers when analyzing applications.

Federal Human Resources (HR) professionals have welcomed CPG's Headline Format-Style Resume for years, and our federal applications have earned thousands of job candidate interviews leading to job offers. These bold headline statements represent relevant, core competen-

cies and skills. They draw attention and make HR representatives want to read more about the experience in order to determine whether the headlines utilized are on the mark.

Think of the federal resume as an advertisement to sell yourself. When writing a federal resume, you'll want to keep it original and let it express everything original about you. However, you want to express that uniqueness in the language of the vacancy announcement. Put yourself in the shoes of the HR Hiring Manager. What will h/she look for in your resume? What specific keywords are in the announcement? What keywords best exemplify your strengths and experience?

For example, if a soldier was an Instructor and Team Leader, the headline might then be "translated" to TRAINING AND LEADERSHIP. If your goal is to become an Aircraft Mechanic, important keywords might be hydraulics, airframe and powerplant, structural repair, operational testing, inspections, or the names of specific tools and equipment used in that profession.

Keep the announcement and your goals in sight at all times, and resist the temptation to highlight non-relevant skills, even if they sound important within the resume. Only knowledge, skills, and abilities relevant to the specific position will be given credit and help qualify you.

Keep it action-oriented and interesting. Show results—especially your individual value and what you bring to a prospective job or organization (again, within the context of the announcement).

Sample Headline Format-Style Resume

Below is an example of how you can use keywords to create headlines within the employment section of a resume. Note how the "headline" is followed by a brief description that captures the key points or accomplishments within the headline and avoids restating job descriptions.

04/2015-09/2017; Director of Emergency Management

PROGRAM MANAGEMENT: Developed and executed budgets up to $300K, supervised up to 10 personnel, and served as one of the lead trainers for new employees, applying management techniques, best practices, and business metrics to evaluate operations and improve efficiency and cost-effectiveness. Served as a senior specialist, evaluating, coordinating, and executing a wide variety of management and administrative services, to include Management and Information Systems (MIS), budget, finance, procurement, personnel, telecommunications, logistics, property, space, records and files, printing and graphics, mail, travel, and office equipment. Provided expert advice on environmental health and safety issues, as well as emergency preparedness and response, including Chemical, Biological, Radiological, Nuclear and (high) Explosive (CBRNE) exercises.

ADMINISTRATIVE/TECHNICAL MANAGEMENT: Oversaw the development, implementation, and evaluation of emergency preparedness programs, analyzing, evaluating, and recommending improvements to achieve effective emergency services. Developed, coordinated, and participated in Table Top Exercise (TTE) and Full Scale Exercise (FSE) training operations as a certified Master Exercise Practitioner (MEP). Employed Homeland Security Exercise and Evaluation Program (HSEEP) methodology to develop training and exercise plans and documentation.

SUBJECT MATTER EXPERT: Advised National Aeronautics and Space Administration (NASA) and U.S. Air Force (USAF) personnel on continuity policy and emergency management policy issues as a key member in a pivotal role overseeing all matters related to emergency preparedness, mitigation, and recovery. Interpreted federal TTE requirements and charts for Agency and Region Emergency Management Working Group members to ensure compliance. Developed and implemented guidance for the design, development, and execution of exercises to enhance emergency response capabilities. Researched and interpreted complex administrative policies and regulations for senior management officials.

EMERGENCY RESPONSE: Coordinated training programs and emergency operations and drills to prepare staff to respond quickly and effectively to emergencies. Participated in numerous emergency operations as a first responder, including industrial accidents such as a Titan-IV A-20 rocket explosion at the Cape Canaveral Air Force Station (CCAFS) in August 1998 (the rocket was carrying a classified payload).

STRATEGIC PLANNING: Applied emergency planning concepts necessary to develop an integrated, generic, comprehensive emergency operations plan and Continuity of Operations (COOP) plan. Provided development and articulation of key policies regarding emergency management. Created strategies and plans for dealing with potential emergency service scenarios.

COMMUNICATIONS: Prepared and delivered correspondence, reports, and presentations. Regularly briefed senior leaders, external stakeholders, and emergency management counterparts on various TTE program aspects. Provide detailed communications and advice on Homeland Security Presidential Directive (HSPD) 20 (National Continuity Policy), HSPD 8 and other federal directives to meet requirements based on NASA and USAF mission, resources, and budget constraints. Served as liaison with other organizations, maintaining positive communications and establishing harmonious working relationships.

ACCOMPLISHMENTS:
*Completed Federal Emergency Management Agency (FEMA) Master Exercise Practitioner certification.
*Disaster Assistance and Rescue Team (DART) member for all-hazard emergency response and recovery.
*Developed and managed a robust emergency management TTE program and COOP.

Step 2. Create (or Modify) the Framework for Your Resume Using the Headline Format

In this step, you simply want to create the overall framework for your resume. We'll finish building the house in the next steps, but first you need to create a blueprint. Remember the keywords you identified in the previous step? Now it's time to drill those down into two to five relevant headlines for each job.

Later, you will add in your duties for each position, and organize them under these headlines. You might use different headlines for different jobs, depending on the position. But your goal is always to organize your duties within relevant headlines, AND to create parallels between your work experience and the duties/qualification of the job for which you're applying.

How Your Resume Builder Might Look at the Completion of Step 2 Using Our Headline Format:

> ### AVIATION MECHANIC
> 173 Pierce Avenue, Macon, GA 31204 United States
> Email: info@careerprocenter.net
> Evening Phone: 478-742-2442
> Day Phone: 478-742-2882
> Highest Federal Civilian Position Held: GS-1670-12

EXPERIENCE:

United States Air Force (USAF)	09/2017 to Present
Charleston Air Force Base (AFB), SC, United States	$40,000 per year
Aviation Lead Technician, WG-8602-10	Average hours per week: 40
Supervisor: Kevin Thomas	Phone: 843-555-3333

Duties, Accomplishments and Related Skills:

LEADERSHIP:

QUALITY ASSURANCE/CONTROL:

AIRCRAFT MAINTENANCE:

TRAINING AND INSTRUCTION:

SELECTED ACCOMPLISHMENTS:
*
*
*
*

You will prepare each job like the one above, going back 10-15 years, and it helps to begin with the same headlines in each job. But as you move through the steps and populate your resume with duties and accomplishments, you may tweak the headlines based on the specific job.

That's fine, but remember that your goal with the headlines is always the same—to create bridges/parallels between the stuff you've done and knowledge you've gained and applied, and the stuff you will be expected to do in the new job.

Think of the karate kid, and the famous "wax on, wax off" scenes. The teacher kept the student moving his hand in a certain way to apply wax to a car, but later, realized that he could use the same muscle memory to block punches and kicks!

Likewise, you want to show how you can use your knowledge and skills to do the job you're targeting, even if it doesn't seem apparent at first.

EDUCATION:

Embry-Riddle Aeronautical University	Major: Professional Aeronautics
Daytona Beach, FL, United States	Minor: Management and Aviation Safety
Bachelor's Degree	GPA: 3.38
Completion Date: 07/2010	127 Semester Credits Earned

Relevant Coursework, Licensures and Certifications:

You don't have to put anything in the box below, but if you feel there are specific courses from your degree that are relevant to the job you're targeting, then go ahead and list 5-10 courses. Similarly, some jobs actually say things like "must have 24 hours of accounting coursework." If that's the case, use the box below to list those courses.

Aircraft Accident Investigation; Aviation Legislation; Aviation Law; Technical Report Writing; English Composition; Introduction to Computers and Applications; Management of Production and Operations; Macroeconomics; Project Management in Aviation Operations

OTHER:
Job Related Training:

RELEVANT TRAINING:
Department of the Interior (DOI), Contracting Officer's Technical Representative (COTR), 06/2017
Flight Safety, Safety System Management, 04/2016
Interagency Committee for Aviation Policy (ICAP) Aviation Safety Officer (ASO), 08/2013
Federal Aviation Administration (FAA) Advanced Aircraft Accident Investigation, 06/2012
Defense Contract Management Agency (DCMA) Aircraft Maintenance Manager, 03/2012
Data Collection and Analysis, 08/2011
Supplier Quality Fundamentals, 07/2011
Intermediate Systems Acquisition, 05/2010
Production, Quality and Manufacturing Fundamentals, 01/2010
Fundamentals of System Acquisition Management, 11/2009
F-117 Engine Bore Scope, 12/2009
C-17A Engine Run Course, 08/2009

Organizations/Affiliations:

American Legion	Member
Toastmasters International	Member

Step 3. Write the Duties and Accomplishments for Each Position

By now, you should have gathered all the information you'll need to write your duties and accomplishments for each position you will include on your resume.

To help you understand the difference between duties and accomplishments, let's use Sergeant Mitchell as an example. He spent five years in the Army as a Signal Support Systems Specialist, which, in Iraq, basically means that he was asked to fix virtually anything with electricity running through it.

The Army has a specific job description for a Signal Support Systems Specialist. These are Sergeant Mitchell's job duties, but they are also the duties of every other Signal Support Systems Specialist in the Army. Mitchell would definitely want to list some duties in his resume, but would need to be careful that they don't sound too generic or vague.

For example, one of the official duties of a Signal Support Systems Specialist in the Army is to "supervise, install, maintain, and troubleshoot signal support systems and terminal devices, to include radio, wire, and battlefield automated systems." What does that mean? Would a civilian hiring manager understand and appreciate that?

Sergeant Mitchell tweaked this language just a little bit to make it work for his resume, taking out some of the military language and making it easier to understand: "Installed, maintained, and provided training and troubleshooting on a variety of secure and non-secure communications systems." This is a simple example, but you can see how this second version is much easier to understand, as well as clearer and more specific.

Accomplishments Are Not Generic. Accomplishments are the specific achievements that YOU did, and improvements YOU made. In Sergeant Mitchell's case, he

did about a million things in Iraq that were unique to his unit, and they work well in his resume.

Here are a couple of specific accomplishments he might list:

Maintained complex radio communications systems for 30 vehicles (worth more than $400K), troubleshooting and replacing equipment, as needed; developed new system for monitoring communications equipment, resulting in zero radio malfunctions during high-intensity combat assignment.

Overcame a lack of internal communications by coordinating with engineers to cut down old telephone poles on abandoned Iraqi facility and to install telephone poles on base; directed installation of aerial telephone wires and tactical phones at key locations, enhancing productivity and overall resources.

Accomplishments are personalized. And remember, you want to include accomplishments that are also relevant. Sergeant Mitchell's accomplishments might help him land a job in the communications field, but as an accountant? Not so much.

Using the Challenge-Context-Action-Result (CCAR) Formula to Write Accomplishments

The key to writing strong accomplishments statements is to answer the question: So what?

Best Practices and Tips for Writing Strong Accomplishments

Focus on Outcome—You'd be amazed by how many people forget to mention this critical aspect of experience. When discussing outcome, be sure to discuss the whats, the hows, and the breadth and scope of your experiences:

What occurred? Did you improve the workplace? Perhaps you refined technology tools, created programs, or organized procedures. Regardless, let the agency know what occurred. Use brief examples to best illustrate your point whenever possible.

How much and how many. Did you start new projects? How many? Did you save the office money? Time? How much? Don't forget percentages, numbers, and degrees that apply.

Notice how this example below falls flat because it ignores the outcome:

As a supervisor at Early Start, oversaw the development of grant proposals. While in this position, put systems in place to ensure employees provided the government with the exact information it needed.

This revision is more revealing—and more competitive:

As a supervisor at Early Start, oversaw team of 10 employees engaged in grant development; developed a template-based system to anticipate requirements and meet deadlines in advance and create proposals that

won two grants over the previous year.

Showcase Your Role—Did you work on your own? As part of a team? In a supervisory capacity? As a team leader? Let the agency know your specific role in the projects. For example, this response ignores the candidate's role(s):

Helped put together conferences. Among responsibilities were sending invitations, calling potential guests, and preparing conference materials.
A stronger way of phrasing would be:

As part of a team of five employees, participated in conference planning; among other responsibilities, coordinated with co-workers to send invitations, contact potential guests, and prepare conference materials.

Were you promoted while working on a project? If so, mention that, too. Note, for example, the following response doesn't mention a promotion:

In last position, spent two to three months at a time in the field collecting samples for the study. The following year, spent most of time in the lab, only going to the field occasionally.

While this revision does mention it:

As Project Manager, spent two to three months at a time

in the field, overseeing five specialists who assisted in the collection of samples for the study. The following year, was promoted to Senior Project Manager, which required more time in the lab and less time in the field.

Remember: Timeframes Count—Be sure to address these questions: What were the dates or time periods you worked on a project or job? Did you work full-time or part-time? If part-time, what percentage of time did you spend perform specific tasks?

For example, this candidate could have worked in his position for a few months as a part-time employee, but the employer won't know for sure:

Served as a contractor for the agency. Regularly produced educational videos and IVT training sessions.

This response is stronger this way:

From 2014 to 2017, served as a full-time contractor for the agency, spending at least 30% of time producing educational videos and IVT training sessions.

If you didn't spend substantial time in a particular position, include the dates anyway. Other information, such as the outcome of your experience or the scope and depth of your work, will underscore its value.

Value Your Experience—Many experiences illuminate your significance as a candidate. For example, you might have published relevant articles or gained valuable experience through:

Leadership positions. Were you president of a sorority or fraternity? Did you lead a team either as part of a classroom experience or a volunteer group? Mention these positions and the outcome of your efforts.

Extracurricular activities. Perhaps you volunteered or belonged to a club that gave you valuable experience.

Let the agency know specific details, including projects, dates, and how that experience applies to the field.

Internships, Training Assignments, and Special Details. Never underestimate the importance of hands-on education, especially internships, whether during the summer or over an entire semester.

Show and Tell—Writing about your experience is great, but be sure to use specific examples, too. For example, read how this candidate's job sounds pretty blasé:

As a Maintenance Mechanic, often work in settings that require strict control of every move in the operation.

Look at the difference a few specifics can make:

As a Maintenance Mechanic, often worked in settings that required strict control of every move in the operation; i.e., for 16 months, worked on renovation projects in the Smithsonian Institution, handling priceless museum exhibits using forklifts, cranes, skids, and rollers.

Writing Tips and Samples

The following tips and examples will demonstrate what you should, and should not, do in your own resume:

Write your resume in the assumed first-person point of view, without using personal pronouns such as "I," "me," or "my."

Poor: *I managed a team of six people in organizing and tracking a major warehouse operation.*

Better: *Directed team of 12 personnel in organizing, tracking, and improving a 24/7 warehouse of trucking supplies valued at more than $800K.*

Use action-based verbs and adjectives, but don't overuse them!

Poor: *Detail-oriented, versatile, results-focused, and dedicated leader with 20 years of experience.*

(uses too many action-oriented adjectives in a row without any specific action verbs that clarify actual tasks)

Better: *Highly skilled Electrical Engineer with 20 years' experience in designing, evaluating, troubleshooting, and improving complex electrical systems for Fortune 500 companies.*

(uses relevant action verbs descriptive of the applicant's tasks)

Write strong accomplishments.

Weak accomplishment: *Manage the supply room and help my section chief organize the armory.*

Better: *Played a key role in organizing and accounting for more than $200K in government inventory; after only one month of preparation, received "Outstanding" rating on official readiness inspection.*

Avoid vague language.

Example of vague language: *Worked with section chief to send tools and equipment to other units in Iraq and the U.S.*

Example of specific language: *Planned logistical movement of 50 different tools and pieces of equipment across international boundaries to support the Global War on Terrorism; more than $1M worth of inventory shipped with 100% accountability.*

In general, choose active voice over passive voice when describing duties and accomplishments.

Example of passive voice with first-person POV: *In Iraq, as part of my responsibilities, hardware and software*

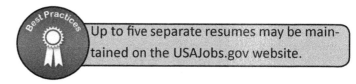

were developed and a help desk was operated.

Example of active voice with assumed first-person POV, without personal pronouns: *Provided expert technical support and customer service while troubleshooting and solving a broad range of Information Technology (IT) problems.*

Step 4. Optimize the "Additional Information" Section

Here at CareerPro Global, we call the "Additional Information" section your "secret weapon." This is because most people don't understand how to use it effectively and often don't use it at all.

However, we have learned over the decades that it's a powerful way to optimize your resume and make it even more relevant and interesting for hiring managers.

Here's the deal. OPM allows candidates to include an additional for 20,000 characters/spaces to include any other information in one's resume that was not already included under Work Experience and Education.

Although it's located at the end of the online system, the "Additional Information" section holds the same weight as anything else, so why not use it to your advantage?

Although none of it is required, here is some of the relevant content you might want to include in this section. The more that applies to you, the better, but don't overdo it and start throwing in random stuff just to provide more content.

While they allow 20,000 characters, we don't recommend using more than 5,000-10,000 characters, tops.

Potential Sections in Additional Information

Security Clearance. List any active or previous security clearances, relevant dates and certifying agency.

Professional Summary. You may want to include a short paragraph that describes your professional experience and skills.

Here is a simple formula for writing a good professional summary:

1. An introductory statement displaying your highest level of qualifications and number of years of work experience. Be specific: "Senior maintenance supervisor with 27 years of progressive experience."

2. Record of improvement/accomplishment: Whenever describing accomplishments, be precise. If possible, quantify the results. For example, you could write, "Reorganized order processing procedures to reduce time required by 30%."

3. Specific skills and training applicable to the job objective.

4. Areas of specialized proficiency (include education level, specialized certifications, and/or security clearances).

5. Work ethic traits demonstrating the skills and experience you bring to the table, and what you can offer to support the organization's mission and operations. (keep this to one sentence)

Career Highlights. Here, you can simply copy/paste three to five of your top accomplishments from throughout the resume. If these include keywords from the job announcement, all the better!

Additional Relevant Experience. If you have positions going back past 10-15 years that you think are relevant, you can list the start and end years, the job title, and the

See the resume samples beginning on page 101 for more ideas and examples on handling the **Additional Information** section.

organization here. You may also want to include a brief summary of your duties/accomplishments.

We don't recommend going back more than 25 years in this summary list. Finally, if you ran out of space in the main work history, you might want to continue a position here if you really think it's relevant.

Honors, Awards, and Recognitions. List the name and month/year received for any awards or honors.

KSAs. If the position includes KSAs and/or core competencies in the resume, we recommend integrating them into the work history. Once you've done that, you can include them here as well. (Learn more about KSAs in Checkpoint 4, on page 55.)

Performance/Rater Comments. Consider listing one to five short excerpts from others who wrote about your performance. These could come from your evaluations, award write-ups—even LinkedIn recommendations.

You can simply put the individuals' first initial and last name, or say something like "cited from 2018 performance appraisal." If possible, choose quotes that are relevant to the position you're targeting.

Relevant Volunteer Work. The government will consider volunteer work as experience in some cases, especially if it's relevant.

However, it's not necessarily a good idea to list volunteer work that's totally unrelated to the job. Also, it's best to avoid including any political or religious information in a federal resume.

Additional Information:

CURRENT SECURITY CLEARANCE: Secret

PROFESSIONAL SUMMARY:

Influential public and government relations/communications professional with more than 10 years of relevant experience. Possess vision for high-return media opportunities and strategies that strengthen organizational position and enhance community recognition. Exceptional ability and knowledge to lead promotional and branding strategy campaigns; and to facilitate complex issues between offices and agencies. Proven ability to influence thinking of others, forge strategic relationships, and build consensus. Now offering versatile skills, broad knowledge, advanced communication abilities, and vast technical expertise to plan and manage robust legislative affairs strategies and programs.

ADDITIONAL KNOWLEDGE, SKILLS, AND ABILITIES:

Demonstrated superior written and oral communication skill in dealing with upper-level management and senior officials. In March 2017, coordinated with government leaders to drive policy changes that would permit the procurement of commercially available satellite weather data. Authored drafts, then shared with key staff members and stakeholders to garner feedback. Updated draft documents and coordinated with leadership for industry-wide dissemination. As a result, helped to establish a new industry that will create thousands of jobs and save millions annually.

ACCOLADES AND PERFORMANCE COMMENTARY:

"[Susan] was integral to our successful engagement on Capitol Hill on our toughest issues."
-cited from 2017 appraisal

"Susan is the consummate public relations expert, and has a comprehensive network of contacts throughout the government, industry and the media."
-cited from 2016 performance award

AWARDS:

*Honored with the 2010 "Award for Meritorious Journalism" for production and delivery of a series of reports on the shortage of childcare services in southern Louisiana.

RELEVANT COMPUTER & TECHNOLOGY SKILLS:

Microsoft Office Suite; digital photography; various web-based editing applications

Equipment/Tools/Systems

Speaking Experience

Publications. List any relevant professional journal articles or books you wrote that were published.

Areas of Expertise (This can simply be a list of "soft skills," such as communication, speaking, and team building. Most importantly, this is yet another opportunity to include some relevant keywords/information from the job announcement that apply to you.)

Step 5. Edit Your Resume

In this final step, it's time to step back a bit and do some quality control. As with any piece of writing, we recommend getting someone else to review, provide feedback, and even offer editorial suggestions.

You might ask a co-worker, mentor, professional writer, or the English major in the family to take a look. The goal is to have a resume that is error-free, grammatically correct, and written in an active voice whenever possible. You should also use Microsoft Word's spelling and grammar check functions.

Finally, you need to check your character counts, and we recommend leaving a "buffer" of at least 100 characters in each field. The USAJOBS character counts have changed over the years, so be sure to check USAJOBS for the most current numbers.

We have included a list below of the allowable characters in the various fields, along with some other helpful guidance. Be sure to check USAJOBS for any changes.

WORK EXPERIENCE:

Employer Name - 60 characters	MM/YYYY to MM/YYYY or Present
Employer Address	$XX,XXX per year
Employer City/Town, State, Zip Code, Country	Average hours per week: XX
Job Title - 100 characters	Federal Grade: XX-XXXX-XX or N/A
Supervisor: Name if OK to contact - 60 characters	Phone: MUST HAVE PHONE - 30 characters

Duties, Accomplishments and Related Skills: [5,000 characters max, including spaces]

Note, if you would like, you can include a brief description of the company or organization's mission for the reader.

HEADLINE:

HEADLINE:

HEADLINE:

ACCOMPLISHMENTS:

*xxxx

*xxxx

*xxxx

Professional Publications: [5,000 characters max, including spaces]

Additional Information: [20,000 characters max, including spaces]

REFERENCES: [No character limit, but keep to 100 characters to prevent formatting errors]

Name
Employer
Title
MUST HAVE PHONE OR REMOVE
Email
Professional or Personal Reference (CHOOSE ONE FROM DROPDOWN LIST)

Developing a Cover Letter

Some federal vacancy announcements allow you to submit a cover letter. If they do, we recommend developing one, as it's yet another tool you can use to convey your relevant experience.

If the vacancy does not ask for or allow a cover letter, do not submit one! Remember, only submit exactly what they ask for: nothing more and nothing less.

A cover letter should be limited to one page, and give the

Use the overall format below as a template to develop your own cover letter.

reader an overview of the following information:

- Why you feel you are a strong candidate for the job
- Your most relevant skills, training, and experience
- A few of your top career accomplishments

RONALD HART
677 Longstreet | Bartlett, Wyoming | 123-456-7890 | anymail@gmail.com

Date

Contact Name
Title
Company
Address
City, State Zip

Dear Sir or Madam:

I am a highly successful land and property acquisition specialist, land owner, licensed real estate agent, and broker with more than three decades of professional success. Further, I have a passion for solving complex land and property management transactions and issues, and believe I am an ideal candidate for the Property Management position.

Please consider the following as a small glimpse into my broad skills and experience:

✓ Formed and led multiagency teams in complex land acquisition and development projects worth more than $800M.

✓ Established a realty company in 2017 and assisted local and regional clients in buying and selling approximately $75M in timber, farm, and commercial properties.

✓ Developed novel approaches to market four timberland properties (20K+ acres) that client had been trying to sell for six years. Sold all properties within six months, creating $17M in net sales for client.

If you are seeking a highly skilled and knowledgeable farm and timberland management expert with an impeccable work ethic and the proven ability to synchronize customer needs with market trends and business goals, please review my attached resume. I would greatly appreciate an opportunity to discuss how I can help to meet and exceed your organization's goals, and I look forward to hearing from you soon.

Sincerely,

Ronald Hart

Susan's Story and Worksheet

Susan used the Headline Format and worked hard to tailor her resume for her targeted position. Below is what she came up with; what follows is what her worksheet would look like.

Susan Jackson
123 Sparse Lane, Ogden, UT 84559
Phone: 123-456-7890
Email: susan@gmail.com

EXPERIENCE:

Global Logistics	10/2013 to Present
222 Apple Orchard Lane	Salary: $95,000 USD per year
Springdale, UT	Average hours per week: 60
Outreach Director	
Supervisor: xxxxx	Phone: xxx-xxx-xxxx; contact: Yes

Duties, Accomplishments and Related Skills:

PUBLIC & LEGISLATIVE AFFAIRS: Plan and direct a program that provided government and public relations support to roughly 40 small and large defense-related technology industry clients doing business with multiple agencies within the Executive Branch. Execute complex, multifaceted appropriation and authorization legislative strategies on an annual and recurring basis, helping corporations seeking to positively influence the Congress. Routinely interact with numerous Members of Congress, including members of all four defense committees and their associated professional staffs.

LEADERSHIP, ADVISING, & DECISION SUPPORT: Direct multifunctional teams on a range of projects and initiatives. Coordinate and facilitate weekly policy and strategy development meetings, along with monthly billing and travel planning and execution. Provide expert advice to senior executives of major defense and space contractors on their annual legislative and business development strategies. Conduct research, conduct analysis, and provide important legislative information and technical advice to inform strategic/corporate decision making.

STRATEGIC/ORGANIZATIONAL AWARENESS & PLANNING: Maintain a keen awareness of key client requirements, interagency relationships, the broad political landscape, the results of various hearings, budget release documentation, and shifting client priorities and constantly sought to align program activities and strategies with overarching strategic goals. Work closely with senior corporate leaders to formulate strategic long-range plans and policies and their associated legislative, outreach, and communication efforts.

REASONING & PROBLEM SOLVING: Utilize sound reasoning to solve complex organizational problems, such as guiding smaller, innovative technology companies through the maze of Executive Branch agencies, providing critical information on documented requirements that their technology could fulfill. Serve as a technical authority on public and governmental affairs among customer agencies. Partnered extensively within individual corporate divisions and business groups to solve problems, coordinate strategy development, and build consensus support for enterprise objectives.

COMMUNICATION & INTERAGENCY COORDINATION: Foster and maintain relationships with senior staff and executives to broaden potential for information and resource sharing. Participate in various issue and policy communication working groups with the White House and Congressional staffs. Work with representatives from various segments of federal, state, local, tribal, and territorial governments as well as the private sector, departmental, and other government entities.

SELECTED ACCOMPLISHMENTS & KEY RESULTS:

*Crafted dozens of impactful strategies to help corporations gain Congressional support and take a role in the government planning and budgeting process.

*Worked closely with major industry manufacturer, resulting in expanded use of Global Positioning System (GPS) technology in both Department of Defense (DOD) and civilian agencies.

*Translated highly technical information and complex issues into short, compelling issue papers, then presented those messages to Members of Congress.

*Demonstrated superior written and oral communication skill in dealing with upper-level management and senior officials. In March 2017, coordinated with government leaders to drive policy changes that would permit the procurement of commercially available satellite weather data. Authored drafts, then shared with key staff members and stakeholders to garner feedback. Updated draft documents and coordinated with leadership for industry-wide dissemination. As a result, helped to establish a new industry that will create thousands of jobs and save millions annually.

*Mentored junior team members to develop their understanding of the budget and appropriations processes, Congressional advocacy, and interagency relationships.

Corporation, Inc.	05/2008 to 09/2013
4444 Crabtree Bridge Way	.
Lafitte, LA	Average hours per week: 60
Public Affairs Specialist	
Supervisor: xxxxx	Phone: xxx-xxx-xxxxx

Duties, Accomplishments and Related Skills:

PUBLIC AFFAIRS & COMMUNICATIONS: Communicated effectively, both verbally and in writing, with a diverse group of stakeholders, senior officials, subordinates interagency, and multinational partners. In absence of the Public Affairs Director, serve as organizational spokesperson. Developed and presented briefings, presentations, and written products on various planning, policy, and operational issues. Prepared concise scripts for broadcast media projects, news releases, opinion pieces, and other media. Interpreted information from different departments, then translated it into effective communications for various stakeholders in appropriate formats.

MEDIA RELATIONS & OUTREACH: Provided a range of written and verbal information to the media and public. Developed outreach programs. Represented organizations in high-level meetings, planning sessions, and other forums with senior executives and Subject Matter Experts (SMEs). Developed and disseminated information through interviews, press releases, newsletters, customer notices, web postings, email-based customer announcements, and social media. Wrote and post syndicated blog entries, including topics of interest, news, and other information, as directed. Actively identified target audiences for specific outreach efforts, including cross-promotional events and partnerships.

SELECTED ACCOMPLISHMENTS & KEY RESULTS:

*Researched, wrote, produced, and edited numerous news items and promotional "teasers" per hour for submission to the groundbreaking "CNN Ticker" broadcast nationally and internationally.

*Responded to hundreds of public information requests via the telephone, Internet, and in writing.

*Researched, wrote, edited, narrated, and produced a special 15-minute video segment on a woman who sought to preserve the area's historical sites.

*Produced and directed weekly, half-hour public affairs program featuring an array of guests and topics for discussion such as the environment and Louisiana state politics. Invited and briefed program guests.

EDUCATION:

University of Montana	Major: Education
Missoula, MT, United States	
Bachelor of Science Degree	GPA: 3.9
Completion Date: 12/2008	
Suma Cum Laude	

OTHER:

Job Related Training:

*Advanced Public Affairs Techniques, 2017
*Integrating Outreach in Strategic Planning, 2017
*Government Relations, 2016
*Journalism, 2016
*Persuasive Writing, 2015
*Introduction to Digital Photography, 2015
*Introduction to Public Affairs, 2012

Additional Information:

CURRENT SECURITY CLEARANCE: Secret

PROFESSIONAL SUMMARY:

Influential public and government relations/communications professional with more than 10 years of relevant experience. Possess vision for high-return media opportunities and strategies that strengthen organizational position and enhance community recognition. Exceptional ability and knowledge to lead promotional and branding strategy campaigns; and to facilitate complex issues between offices and agencies. Proven ability to influence thinking of others, forge strategic relationships, and build consensus. Now offering versatile skills, broad knowledge, advanced communication abilities, and vast technical expertise to plan and manage robust legislative affairs strategies and programs.

ADDITIONAL KNOWLEDGE, SKILLS, AND ABILITIES:

Demonstrated superior written and oral communication skill in dealing with upper-level management and senior officials. In March 2017, coordinated with government leaders to drive policy changes that would permit the procurement of commercially available satellite weather data. Authored drafts, then shared with key staff members and stakeholders to garner feedback. Updated draft documents and coordinated with leadership for industry-wide dissemination. As a result, helped to establish a new industry that will create thousands of jobs and save millions annually.

ACCOLADES AND PERFORMANCE COMMENTARY:

"[Susan] was integral to our successful engagement on Capitol Hill on our toughest issues."
-cited from 2017 appraisal

"Susan is the consummate public relations expert, and has a comprehensive network of contacts throughout the government, industry and the media."
-cited from 2016 performance award

AWARDS:

*Honored with the 2010 "Award for Meritorious Journalism" for production and delivery of a series of reports on the shortage of childcare services in southern Louisiana.

RELEVANT COMPUTER & TECHNOLOGY SKILLS:

Microsoft Office Suite; digital photography; various web-based editing applications

CareerPro Global
YOUR CAREER IS OUR BUSINESS®

Roadmap to Federal Jobs Worksheet

Instructions: This worksheet is designed to use each time you apply for a federal job. It's best to follow the checkpoints in order, and don't move on until you complete all the steps in a given checkpoint. Once you apply for a job and begin preparing for the interview, simply go back to checkpoint 1 and start again with your next application. Cast a wide net and follow the best practices in the book, and you should eventually find the perfect federal job for you! And remember, you can always refer back to the Roadmap to Federal Jobs book for more detailed information in each area.

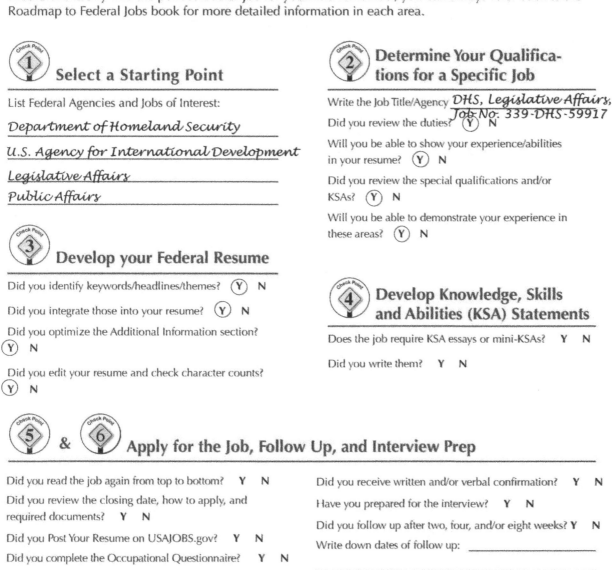

① Select a Starting Point

List Federal Agencies and Jobs of Interest:

Department of Homeland Security

U.S. Agency for International Development

Legislative Affairs

Public Affairs

② Determine Your Qualifications for a Specific Job

Write the Job Title/Agency *DHS, Legislative Affairs, Job No. 339-DHS-59917*

Did you review the duties? (Y) N

Will you be able to show your experience/abilities in your resume? (Y) N

Did you review the special qualifications and/or KSAs? (Y) N

Will you be able to demonstrate your experience in these areas? (Y) N

③ Develop your Federal Resume

Did you identify keywords/headlines/themes? (Y) N

Did you integrate those into your resume? (Y) N

Did you optimize the Additional Information section? (Y) N

Did you edit your resume and check character counts? (Y) N

④ Develop Knowledge, Skills and Abilities (KSA) Statements

Does the job require KSA essays or mini-KSAs? Y N

Did you write them? Y N

⑤ & ⑥ Apply for the Job, Follow Up, and Interview Prep

Did you read the job again from top to bottom? Y N

Did you review the closing date, how to apply, and required documents? Y N

Did you Post Your Resume on USAJOBS.gov? Y N

Did you complete the Occupational Questionnaire? Y N

Write the date you applied & the job title and #

_____

_____

Did you receive written and/or verbal confirmation? Y N

Have you prepared for the interview? Y N

Did you follow up after two, four, and/or eight weeks? Y N

Write down dates of follow up: _____

_____

Assembling a Best Qualified Federal Resume

7 Federal Resume Tips That Produce Interviews and Jobs

Writing a great resume is like putting together a jigsaw puzzle. It involves both art and science. Art and creativity are needed to turn a dry document into something that hiring decision makers find appealing, interesting, and readable.

The science is more practical; it's the specific information that indicates your qualifications for the position to both machines (applicant tracking systems) and humans.

The intentional and thoughtful combination of the art and science components—the way the puzzle pieces fit together—will get your resume read and lead to interviews that lead to job offers.

Like a jigsaw puzzle, creating a standout resume for a federal job can be complicated and time consuming. With corporate resumes, there's pressure to pack an entire career's worth of information into a cramped space (two pages of 11-point font).

It's still necessary to be concise when writing a federal resume, but the challenge involves precision more than compression. There are plenty of pieces to a federal resume, and they must fit together in a fashion that's coherent and makes your unique qualifications immediately evident.

The Devil is in the Details

Anyone who has glanced at an opening on USAJOBS knows that the position descriptions found there can be lengthy, with detailed qualifications that a candidate must meet to qualify for the job. The initial sort of applicants for most federal positions is based on a structured set of criteria included in the position description.

For you to be considered for the position, your experience, background, and credentials must meet the prerequisites. You'll have to provide the details; the process is designed to weed out applicants who can't follow instructions. If you don't meet the criteria and include all of the specifics required, your application will wind up in the digital trash.

Assuming that none of the components is missed and you meet the qualifications for the position, your application undergoes a second evaluation and is rated and categorized according to how closely it meets the criteria for the position:

Best Qualified: Applicants with a background that closely matches the evaluation criteria (95% - 100% match).

Well Qualified: Applicants with experience who satisfactorily meet the criteria (85% - 94% match).

Qualified: Applicants with the basic qualifications, general knowledge, skills, and abilities (70% - 84% match).

It's easy to guess which category is most likely to get an interview and receive an offer, so the obvious question is, how do you write an interview that is likely to receive a "Best Qualified" rating?

7 Steps to Produce a "Best Qualified" Resume

How much qualitative difference actually exists between the top 5% of candidates and the top 15% or the top 25%? Some, but it's equally likely that extremely Well Qualified candidates may fall into the lower qualification levels simply because their capabilities aren't clearly communicated.

Getting the edge in a tight competitive field may come from the way your information focuses on the key requirements and how easy you make it for decision makers to recognize your fit for the position.

Here are seven steps to help you piece together the Federal Resume puzzle:

1. Read the job announcement, then read it again!

Make a list of the requirements for the position. Look through the body of the position description, including the overview and the job requirements. Make sure to click the according boxes on the right to review application and document requirements.

You'll also want to take a look at links to any application forms or questionnaires required as part of the application. **Make a checklist and review it before submitting your application.**

2. Analyze the keywords.

The keywords used in the position description are your best clue for the words that will be used for automated selection by applicant tracking systems and for what human readers will be looking for. Again, make a list. You'll want to use the most prominent keywords in your resume and application responses.

3. Customize each resume for the position.

While it makes sense to work from a master resume that includes descriptions and stories that you've developed to emphasize your experience and capabilities, you'll want to structure a new resume for each application. Use the online resume builder to write each resume. You'll also be able to save and recall the resumes, as needed, to re-customize for other positions.

4. Keep it relevant.

Emphasize information and narratives that meet the position requirements. Leave out activities that don't clearly relate. Few agencies specifically require

Knowledge, Skills, and Abilities (KSA) statements as part of the resume packages, but there may be questionnaires that require the same kind of information.

At CareerPro Global, we typically develop "mini KSAs" that are included in the resume and in the Additional Experience section of the USAJOBS resume builder. These short narratives reinforce questionnaire responses by integrating KSA information within the body of the resume. Keep the language relevant and clear, especially if you're making a transition from the military. Avoid acronyms, jargon, and "resume speak."

5. Keep it concise.

Federal resumes can run five pages or more, but you'll want to keep your information concise and easy to scan. Key information should jump off the page. If a decision maker can't scan your resume in 10-15 seconds and quickly identify your capabilities, then you'll need to make some edits and revisions.

6. Emphasize accomplishments, avoid descriptions.

Traditional job descriptions don't convey your contributions. You'll want to use short narratives or

stories that illustrate results and achievements. CareerPro uses a CCAR format that describes Challenges, Context, Actions, and Results to link descriptive narratives to the capabilities and knowledge required in the position description.

7. Submit the application and all the supporting documents on time.

Double- and triple-check the USAJOBS description. Make sure that you submit SF-50 forms, transcripts, and other documentation listed, as requirements. Also pay attention to the closing date at the top of the description.

While faxed and mailed applications may be permitted, most agencies prefer online applications; you'll want to submit your resume, documents, and questionnaires online, unless there are specific instructions to do otherwise.

Checkpoint Notes

Checkpoint Notes

Checkpoint 4

Knowledge, Skills, and Abilities (KSA) Statements and Occupational Questionnaires

KNOWLEDGE, SKILLS, AND ABILITIES (KSA) STATEMENTS AND OCCUPATIONAL QUESTIONNAIRES

WHAT ARE KSAS AND CORE COMPETENCIES?

KSAs are simply knowledge, skills, and abilities that the hiring agency has deemed important to perform the job. All the following guidance also applies to "core competencies" that may be included in the vacancy announcement. For many years, federal applicants had to not only submit a resume, but also submit one- to two-page KSA essays as part of the hiring process.

However, as a part of the federal-wide Hiring Reform initiative in recent years, approximately 90% of federal agencies have eliminated the requirement of narrative KSAs from the initial application in the hiring process.

Still, many jobs still include KSAs as optional (think of it as extra credit in a college course—yes, you want the extra credit!), or ask you to represent them in the resume, and/or require short responses to an occupational questionnaire.

Here's an example from a vacancy announcement posted in spring 2018:

How You Will Be Evaluated

You will be evaluated for this job based on how well you meet the qualifications above.

Human Resources (HR) will review resumes and transcript(s) to ensure applicants meet the ba[sic] qualification requirements. HR will evaluate each applicant who meets the basic qualification[s] the information provided in the assessment questionnaire. The assessment questionnaire wil[l] take approximately 30 minutes to complete. Applicants determined best qualified will be refe[rred] to the selecting official.

Applicants will be further evaluated on the following "Knowledge, Skills, and Abilities (KSAs)" through your resume and responses to the online questions:

1. Ability to interpret and apply Federal laws, regulations and policies as they relate to the management of: real property; personal property; personal property disposal; motor vehicles[;] heavy equipment; nonexpendable property; records management; library functions; and qua[lity] management.

2. Ability to provide coordination of a program which may include persuasion of groups with diverse objectives. Provide Property Management expertise on FSSI, GSA Advantage, and FBM[S].

3. Skill in written communication to provide technical information and written policy and

---

What Are Occupational Questionnaires?

Occupational questionnaires are simply online question- naires included in the application process. Sometimes you'll find only basic questions regarding Veterans' Pref- erence or other information. Then again, the question- naire can be quite lengthy and specific with job-related questions.

In these cases, you will most likely NOT be required to provide an essay/narrative response for each KSA, but will instead be required to answer multiple-choice ques- tions and essentially rate yourself from "no experience" to "expert."

While you must be completely honest and transparent in your answers, as well as be able to back them up in the resume and interview, it's best to show as much experi- ence as possible.

Your online assessment will be closely cross-referenced with your resume to ensure your work history supports your answers with substantial evidence of your posses-

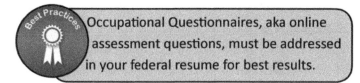
Occupational Questionnaires, aka online assessment questions, must be addressed in your federal resume for best results.

sion of each KSA. These should be specific examples that clearly reflect the highest level of your ability.

If you don't provide this support in your resume, your nu- merical rating score may be adjusted; you could even be eliminated from consideration if Human Resources (HR) staff don't see a match between your answers in the on- line questionnaire and your resume.

Likewise, sometimes the occupational questionnaire will provide a field for a brief narrative response, such as "If you answered 'D' to the question above, please provide a specific example/please indicate where this experience is reflected in your resume."

The following is an excerpt from an occupational ques- tionnaire on USAJOBS.gov:

---

1. Select the one statement that best describes the experience that you possess that demonstrates your ability to perform the work of a Logistics Management Specialist at the GS-12 grade level or equivalent pay band in the Federal Service.

- A. I have one year of specialized experience equivalent to the GS-11 grade level in the Federal service which includes: performing studies and analysis of policies and procedures of property accountability; updating supply policies for the organization to meet requirements of higher authority; providing advice in resolving problems of logistics and equipment management.

- B. My experience is not reflected in the above statement.

Select the one statement that most accurately describes your training and experience carrying out each task using the scale provided.

2. Analyze property accountability policies to ensure compliance with established regulations.

- A. I have not had education, training, or experience in performing this task.

- B. I have had education or training in how to perform this task, but have not yet performed it on the job.

- C. I have performed this task on the job. My work on this task was monitored closely by a supervisor or senior employee to ensure compliance with proper procedures.

- D. I have performed this task as a regular part of a job. I have performed it independently and normally without review by a supervisor or senior employee.

- E. I am considered an expert in performing this task. I have supervised performance of this task or am normally the person who is consulted by other workers to assist or train them in doing this task because of my expertise.

Incorporating KSA Responses into the Resume

Whether in the work history, or in the occupational questionnaire fields, or both, the presence of "mini" KSA responses is integral to HR staff members' ability to determine whether candidates meet the basic qualifications of the position, and whether they are found to be Best Qualified.

Candidates who are selected for the interview process will have to defend their statements in an interview and possibly provide even more details. With this in mind, you must thoroughly explain what you have accomplished and how you did so in a little "story."

They should be included as accomplishments in the corresponding job, which means the KSAs should be as current/recent/relevant as possible (ideally from the past 5-10 years).

Once you ensure all KSAs are clearly addressed in the work history, you can also include them in the "Additional Information" section of your resume and simply create the heading "Additional Knowledge, Skills, and Abilities."

How to Write a Strong KSA Essay

We recommend that you present your KSA responses in a concise paragraph of maybe four to eight lines, in the same **Challenge-Context-Action-Result (CCAR)** format you used to write your career accomplishments.

Here it is again:

Challenge: Describe a specific problem or goal.

Context: Talk about the individuals and groups with whom you worked, and/or the environment in which you worked, to tackle a particular challenge (e.g., clients, co-workers, Members of Congress, shrinking budget, low morale).

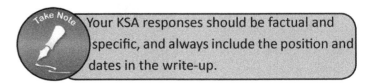

Your KSA responses should be factual and specific, and always include the position and dates in the write-up.

Action: Discuss the specific actions you took to address a challenge.

Result: Give specific examples of the results of your actions. These accomplishments demonstrate the quality and effectiveness of your leadership skills.

Let's look at an example featuring a "before-and-after" written narrative statement for the following KSA:

Ability to develop clear, concise, and accurate written materials for wide dissemination.

> **BEFORE:** I have written numerous policies, letters, and memoranda. These written documents cover a variety of complex topics and I have never had a complaint from a reader. I am a good writer and pride myself on my creativity and writing skills and never suffer from writer's block. My work is always grammatically correct and there are no spelling errors.

The above is a somewhat weak example, because it's basic and vague, it doesn't tell a story, and it doesn't differentiate the candidate from the rest of the applicant pool. There is nothing specific or especially noteworthy in this example.

Now let's take a look at the "After," which uses the CCAR format:

AFTER:

While I was serving as an HR Specialist (GS-12) within the Department of Army's Transportation Command from 05/2016 to 12/2017, I wrote policies and procedures on performance management, staffing, and employee relations affecting more than 5,000 personnel [Challenge/Context].

When an external audit identified serious deficiencies in the agency's personnel policies, I wrote new policies to address those issues and correct misunderstandings about performance management **[Action]**. As a result, I received a performance award, and was recently asked to discuss the policies at a high-level HR meeting. The policies I developed were later implemented across the Department of Defense. **[Result].**

In this second example, you can see the CCAR (highlighted) of the story and how it demonstrates the applicant's specific experience in writing. It accomplishes this task in just under 700 characters (including spaces).

If you don't have a specific work-related situation to include, you can try a few other approaches, as follows:

Education/Training Narrative
This example puts more of a focus on knowledge acquired through formal education or professional enrichment opportunities.

The following is a statement of related education and training that supports the narrative. The employee is Chief of Medical Technical Equipment, GS-12.

Knowledge of the mission, organization, and activities of a healthcare facility.

Education and Specialized Training: Currently enrolled (with 42 hours earned) in dual-degree Bachelor's program at Howard University, Washington, D.C., in Business Management and Computer Sciences. Earned well above 1,500 hours training with advanced medical technology and equipment. In earlier career, completed more than 400 hours as a Firefighter in fire safety, prevention, and emergency medical care.

Award/Recognition Narrative
An award or recognition indicates the quality of experience performed that demonstrates a specific skill, knowledge, or ability. The record of the award must contain sufficient information about relevant behaviors or activities to show that the KSA was demonstrated at some level. The following statement was written by an Environmental Specialist, GS-13.

Knowledge of federal Hazardous Materials (HAZMAT) transportation regulations.

At the conclusion of a recent Safety Review by the Federal Motor Carrier Safety Administration (FMCSA) in 08/2017, I was commended for my knowledge of regulations and programs developed for the company. In addition, on my most recent performance evaluation, I was cited for having "excelled at meeting new challenges and improving the performance of the Fleet Safety Programs."

While we haven't seen very many "traditional" or "full" KSAs in recent years, some agencies do still use them.

If they do require separate essays, read the job announcement, check out the occupational questionnaire, and/or email the HR contact to find out if there is a page limit (usually one to two pages max), or a text box with a character/word count.

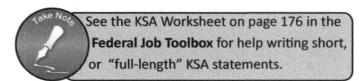

See the KSA Worksheet on page 176 in the **Federal Job Toolbox** for help writing short, or "full-length" KSA statements.

Here are some KSAs from a Department of the Interior announcement in Spring 2018, seeking a GS-5 General Supply Specialist:

Required Documents

To be considered for this position, applicants must submit a cover letter, resume with salary history, and their recent performance evaluation by mail or email.

In addition, applicants must prepare a concise narrative addressing EACH of the Knowledge, Skills, and Abilities (KSA's) listed below to determine the extent to which your application shows that you possess the KSA's associated with this position. Responses should be typed on a separate document. When describing your knowledge, skills, and abilities, please be sure to give examples and explain how often you used these skills, the complexity of the knowledge you possessed, the level of the individuals you interacted with, the sensitivity of the issues you handled, etc. The information provided in your KSA responses will be heavily relied upon in the rating process. Show how your experience and/or education provided you with the KSA.

1. Please detail your experience in contracting for and/or purchasing goods and services on behalf of an organization.
2. Describe your ability and experience in keeping information organized.
3. Please explain your ability to coordinate activities, manage workflow, establish priorities and meet deadlines.

Susan's Story and Worksheet

Susan only had one KSA in the job announcement, so she included an accomplishment in her current job that clearly addressed the question. Her integrated KSA statement is below:

Demonstrated superior written and oral communication skill in dealing with upper-level management and senior officials. In March 2017, coordinated with government leaders to drive policy changes that would permit the procurement of commercially available satellite weather data. Authored drafts, then shared with key staff members and stakeholders to garner feedback. Updated draft documents and coordinated with leadership for industry-wide dissemination. As a result, helped to establish a new industry that will create thousands of jobs and save millions annually.

On the next page is how her worksheet would look like so far.

CareerPro Global
YOUR CAREER IS OUR BUSINESS®

Roadmap to Federal Jobs Worksheet

Instructions: This worksheet is designed to use each time you apply for a federal job. It's best to follow the checkpoints in order, and don't move on until you complete all the steps in a given checkpoint. Once you apply for a job and begin preparing for the interview, simply go back to checkpoint 1 and start again with your next application. Cast a wide net and follow the best practices in the book, and you should eventually find the perfect federal job for you! And remember, you can always refer back to the Roadmap to Federal Jobs book for more detailed information in each area.

1 Select a Starting Point

List Federal Agencies and Jobs of Interest:

Department of Homeland Security

U.S. Agency for International Development

Legislative Affairs

Public Affairs

3 Develop your Federal Resume

Did you identify keywords/headlines/themes? (Y) N

Did you integrate those into your resume? (Y) N

Did you optimize the Additional Information section?
(Y) N

Did you edit your resume and check character counts?
(Y) N

2 Determine Your Qualifications for a Specific Job

Write the Job Title/Agency *DHS, Legislative Affairs, Job No. 339-DHS-59917*
Did you review the duties? (Y) N

Will you be able to show your experience/abilities in your resume? (Y) N

Did you review the special qualifications and/or KSAs? (Y) N

Will you be able to demonstrate your experience in these areas? (Y) N

4 Develop Knowledge, Skills and Abilities (KSA) Statements

Does the job require KSA essays or mini-KSAs? (Y) N

Did you write them? (Y) N

5 & 6 Apply for the Job, Follow Up, and Interview Prep

Did you read the job again from top to bottom? Y N

Did you review the closing date, how to apply, and required documents? Y N

Did you Post Your Resume on USAJOBS.gov? Y N

Did you complete the Occupational Questionnaire? Y N

Write the date you applied & the job title and #

_____

_____

_____

Did you receive written and/or verbal confirmation? Y N

Have you prepared for the interview? Y N

Did you follow up after two, four, and/or eight weeks? Y N

Write down dates of follow up: _____

_____

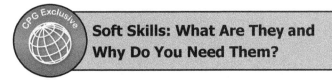

Soft Skills: What Are They and Why Do You Need Them?

You've surely heard the term before and you probably have some idea of what "soft skills" are. Over the past few years, people-oriented soft skills have been a hot topic in the HR community.

To be more precise, HR folks talk a lot about the difficulty of finding candidates that possess soft skills along with the requisite "hard" technical knowledge they need to succeed.

Let's give the phrase a solid definition. Soft skills fall into six specific categories:

1. Communications: Active listening skills, and the ability to speak and to write with an emphasis on conveying ideas and opinions in a clear, professional, and polite manner.

2. Decision making and problem solving: The ability to analyze and make a determination. This category also includes creativity, abstract thinking, and the ability to learn from experience (and from mistakes).

3. Self-management: The initiative required for effective work. Self-management skills include efficiency, a sense of urgency, the ability to adapt, working well under pressure and deadlines, and the ethical standards that govern personal behavior and interactions with others.

4. Teamwork: The ability to work and play well with others. Teamwork strengths include responsibility, accountability, and the ability to share ideas in a way that's positive and encouraging.

5. Professionalism: The characteristics that govern the quality of relationships with customers, peers, and managers. Attributes of professionalism also include

the ability to accept direction and the sensitivity demonstrated in difficult business or personal situations.

6. Leadership: Capability to see the big picture and to manage change. Leadership traits include the willingness both to lead and to follow and the ability to motivate others.

Soft Skills and Emotional Intelligence

The definition of the six categories of "soft skills" make it easy to understand why they're considered important. Soft skills describe the attributes of successful and productive employees and leaders. But there's another important reason that you should focus on development of these characteristics:

85% of your financial success is due to your personality and ability to communicate, negotiate, and lead. Only 15% is due to technical knowledge.

This statistic stems originally from research conducted in 1918 at Carnegie Mellon by physicist and engineer Charles Riborg Mann. It has gained currency with more recent studies and research in a newer area that is termed *Emotional Intelligence.*

The phrase was coined by two researchers, Peter Salavoy and John Mayer, and popularized by psychologist Daniel Goleman in his 1995 book with the same name

(*Emotional Intelligence*). In the book, Goleman defines an Emotional Intelligence Quotient (EQ) as a measure of a set of skills that include "control of one's impulses, self-motivation, empathy, and social competence in interpersonal relationships."

There's an obvious relationship between Emotional Intelligence and soft skills. Essentially, it's Emotional Intelligence that enables the soft skills characteristics.

According to Goleman, an individual needs an Intelligence Quotient (IQ) of 115, only slightly above average, to master the technical knowledge needed to be a doctor, lawyer, or business executive. Once people enter the workforce, IQ and technical skills are often similar among those on the same career path. Emotional Intelligence is the differentiator that determines who moves up the ladder.

The major difference between IQ and EQ is that EQ can be developed. Emotional Intelligence can be learned behavior. In an article for the Harvard Extension School blog, Laura Wilcox explains that development of EQ involves conditioned management of the interaction between the emotional and the cognitive sides of our brains.

Because emotions are instinctive, wrapped up with survival reactions, they occur more rapidly than the rational analysis of the cognitive side of the brain. When the cognitive side can't keep up, emotions can "hijack our ability to reason."

Developing EQ involves controlling our ability to manage emotional encounters, as well as development of techniques to avoid triggering "emotional hijacks" in the people we associate with. Increasing your Emotional Intelligence is both a matter of self-control and a conscious process that affirms the emotional needs of others.

Soft skills and Emotional Intelligence are closely intertwined. It's easy to understand that people with high EQ are more likely to have well-developed communication, teamwork, and leadership skills.

The Soft Skills Gap

Businesses and organizations value soft skills. A 2014 CareerBuilder survey of 2,138 hiring managers and HR professionals found that 77% believe that soft skills are just as important as technical competencies. The chart below shows the 10 soft skills most valued by employers: Soft skills are in high demand but potentially short supply. 2016 research by economist Guy Berger, Ph.D., indicates that U.S. hiring managers are experiencing a "soft skills shortage."

In Berger's survey, 59% of hiring managers responded that soft skills were difficult to find, while 53% experienced difficulty sourcing "hard" technical skills. 58% of respondents indicated that lack of soft skills among candidates is "limiting their company's productivity."

Top 10 Most In-Demand Soft Skills
(Based on % of members with skill who were hired into a new job)

1	Communication	57.9%
2	Organization	56.5%
3	Teamwork	56.4%
4	Always Punctual	55.9%
5	Critical Thinking	55.8%
6	Social Skills	55.8%
7	Creativity	55.0%
8	Interpersonal Communication	55.0%
9	Adaptability	54.9%
10	Friendly Personality	54.6%

Source: Guy Berger, Ph.D.

Another fascinating report, commissioned by McDonald's in the UK, examined the value of soft skills to the UK economy and the potential impact of a "soft skills deficit":

We estimate that over half a million (535,000) UK workers will be significantly held back by soft skills deficits by 2020, an issue expected to affect all sectors of the economy. In absolute terms, the accommodation and food services, retail, and health and social work sectors will be most affected.

The annual overall expected loss of production due to expected soft skills deficits is anticipated to amount to just under £8.4 billion per year by 2020.

If the current weaknesses in the UK's soft skills base are not addressed, we face an economic penalty that will impact on sectors, businesses, individuals, and society as a whole.

To tackle this, individuals, businesses, education institutions, and [policymakers] should take action to [recognize] and promote soft skills.

There is a direct connection between soft skills and the Key Performance Indicators that are important to business—productivity, efficiency, quality of products and service, and, ultimately, revenue and profits. Technical skills are certainly required for organizations to succeed, but factoring soft skills into the hiring equation makes good economic sense for employers.

How Do You Communicate Your Soft Skills?

It's also clear that exercising your Emotional Intelligence Quotient (EQ) can give you a career advantage. Soft skills are in demand, and you'll certainly want to emphasize them if you're making a career move. There's a problem, though.

Announcing that you have a high EQ during a job interview won't go over well. In fact, it probably demonstrates that you lack EQ. Likewise, you might not want to add a "soft skills" section to your resume. It may be true that you work and play well with others, but somehow the statement doesn't fit in a list of core competencies. It just sounds like bragging.

A better strategy **demonstrates** EQ and soft skills with the stories you tell, specifically in the narratives you use to describe your accomplishments in your resume and interviews. Let's look at a short example that could be included in a corporate resume:

> Successfully coached team leaders to improve understanding and utilization of new quality management system. Negotiated objections and created enthusiasm for the program by illustrating efficiency benefits to individual workers, increases in team productivity, and 11% reduction in manufacturing waste.

The bullet point is two sentences, but it tells a clear story of how the candidate championed a new quality management system. The results are there, and soft skills are emphasized—coaching, negotiating, and creating enthusiasm.

Federal hiring is mostly suspended at present, but soft skills and EQ will be in demand when agencies are eventually allowed to fill vacancies. For SES jobs, language that demonstrates soft skills fits naturally into the required ECQ definitions. Narratives that demonstrate soft skills should also be included in the body of USAJOBS resumes.

You'll also want to rehearse your stories for interviews. The way you express yourself verbally provides a direct example of your communication skills. Make sure to weave examples of teamwork, problem-solving skills, and creativity into your narratives.

Checkpoint Notes

Checkpoint Notes

Checkpoint 5

Apply for the Job and Follow Up

APPLY FOR THE JOB AND FOLLOW UP

Understanding the Application Process

The federal government's hiring process is quite different from that of the private sector due to the many laws, Executive Orders (EOs), and regulations that govern federal employment. The federal government has its own language, application, and requirements. Applicants must understand and follow all requirements in order to be successful.

Here at CareerPro Global, we have assisted more than 60,000 people in applying for federal jobs. Just to give you an idea of what's involved, one of our Master Federal Career Advisors helps our clients to target a specific job or series of job.

Next, one of our professional writers spends anywhere from 8-20 or more hours coaching the client, asking relevant and job-specific questions, developing the resume, and then working with the client to make any final revisions.

If there are KSAs involved or other special application needs, the process may take even longer.

So, while we strive to make it as simple as possible, the process tends to be much more robust than a typical hiring process in the private sector.

Not only are the positions very competitive, but the resumes are also longer and more detailed than the standard one or two-page private-sector resume.

Earning the highest rating doesn't automatically guarantee that you'll receive an interview. Sometimes, the announcement can be unexpectedly canceled.

Sometimes the candidate pool can be limited to allow only a small number of people to be referred to the hiring official for an interview.

Maybe the selected pool all had Veterans' Preference, while you didn't. Just remember, at some point, every single government employee had to apply from outside the government. If they can do it, you can, too!

Other Application Systems

Most federal positions begin the hiring process through the USAJOBS.gov portal, and there are many tutorials and other types of support on the site. In some instances, you may be directed to an agency-specific system, such as that of the Federal Aviation Administration (FAA).

Likewise, agencies such as NASA use the USAJOBS, but enforce very specific character limitations (32,200 total, with spaces). Usually, your USAJOBS resume will just "follow" your application automatically through the process. But, as part of your preparation and research before you apply for the job, be sure to check the agency's site for any unique requirements—or formatting, length, or character restrictions.

Steps to Determine Your Qualifications

The Human Resources (HR) Review Process for determining your qualifications and for rating as follows:

Step 1: Application Review

A Personnel Staffing Specialist will review the application package to make sure it has been correctly completed and includes all the appropriate documentation requested (many people don't progress beyond this point).

If the application is complete and correct, the Personnel Staffing Specialist will review the resume to decide if you possess the basic qualifications for the position, in accordance with the Qualifications Handbook. HR will also ensure applicants possess any required Selective Placement Factors (SPFs).

Step 2: Resume Review

The Staffing Specialist will then review the application to determine whether you meet the specialized experience qualifications for the job. This qualification information can be found on every vacancy announcement.

Occupational questionnaires and any narrative statements will also be reviewed for both the quality of response (whether the applicant answered a question indicating that h/she had basic knowledge or expert knowledge, for example) and to ensure answers to questions are supported by the resume (an applicant did not simply mark "expert" in all cases with nothing supporting that answer in the resume).

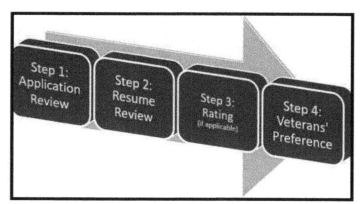

Step 3: Rating (if applicable)

Resumes, questionnaires, and short narrative statements will be reviewed by the HR staff or a panel of Subject Matter Experts (SMEs) and assigned to a rating category using a crediting plan or "scorecard."

Candidates will be placed in one of three categories, generally called "Best Qualified," "Well Qualified," and "Qualified." Each level has a description of benchmarks, which are examples of tasks a candidate would perform at that level.

Agencies may emphasize the most important aspects of a job by assigning relative weights to each factor considered. Once the review is complete, all applicants will be placed in the appropriate category.

Step 4: Veterans' Preference

Applicants with preference eligibility are provided with that "credit." Candidates with 10-point preference are generally placed in the top category; candidates with 5-point eligibility are placed in their assigned category.

Only candidates in the highest category may be referred to the hiring manager. Non-veterans in a category may not be selected over veteran candidates in that same category.

Applying for Specific Jobs

Now that you've developed your resume offline, it's time to log into your USAJOBS account (or create one), and

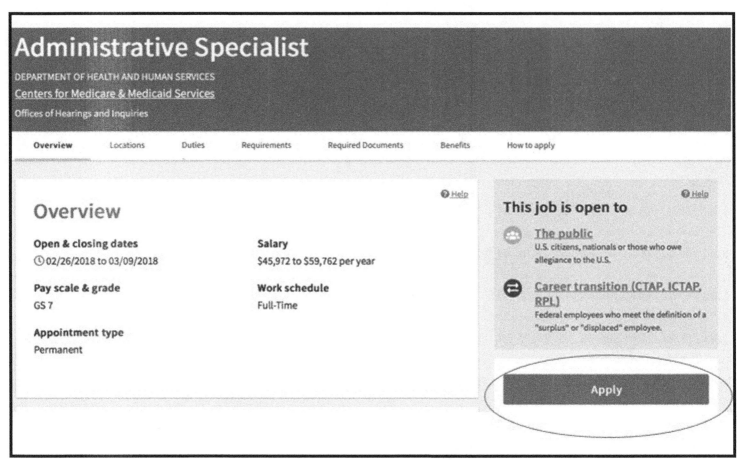

then copy/paste all your great content into their online resume builder. Once you've done that, you're ready to start applying for jobs!

To get started, you simply find the job announcement you're interested in on USAJOBS.gov, and then click on the "Apply" button. You will then be asked to select your resume from a list, and then the system will guide you through the application process.

Sometimes, this includes an occupational questionnaire, and sometimes this process includes uploading other career documents, such as performance appraisals or transcripts.

Next, you should receive some kind of written confirmation (usually automated) confirming that your application was accepted. If you don't receive this, it's best to call the contact on the vacancy and ask for confirmation.

Similarly, if you have any questions or problems about the application process, use the contact info on the vacancy. You can then track your applications within your USAJOBS profile, and should receive updates from the hiring agency about whether you're selected for further review, or for an interview.

Follow Up

What if you don't hear back in a timely manner? It's a good idea to apply for as many positions as possible, and check in at least weekly on your USAJOBS account to monitor your status.

If you don't receive a response from a given agency within four to six weeks, you can certainly contact the representative on the announcement, and ask for an update.

They may or may not be willing or able to provide details. Patience is important here, because some vacancies are filled quite rapidly and efficiently, while others drag out for many months.

If you're not selected for a position, you can ask for feedback on your application.

Again, you may or may not receive the level of detail or feedback you desire; it just depends on the agency and individual with which you're dealing.

Susan's Story and Worksheet

As we check in with Susan, she has applied for the job and received a confirmation email. Turn the page to see what her worksheet would look like so far.

CareerPro Global
YOUR CAREER IS OUR BUSINESS®

Roadmap to Federal Jobs Worksheet

Instructions: This worksheet is designed to use each time you apply for a federal job. It's best to follow the checkpoints in order, and don't move on until you complete all the steps in a given checkpoint. Once you apply for a job and begin preparing for the interview, simply go back to checkpoint 1 and start again with your next application. Cast a wide net and follow the best practices in the book, and you should eventually find the perfect federal job for you! And remember, you can always refer back to the Roadmap to Federal Jobs book for more detailed information in each area.

(1) Select a Starting Point

List Federal Agencies and Jobs of Interest:

Department of Homeland Security

U.S. Agency for International Development

Legislative Affairs

Public Affairs

(2) Determine Your Qualifications for a Specific Job

Write the Job Title/Agency *DHS, Legislative Affairs, Job No. 339-DHS-59917*

Did you review the duties? **(Y)** N

Will you be able to show your experience/abilities in your resume? **(Y)** N

Did you review the special qualifications and/or KSAs? **(Y)** N

Will you be able to demonstrate your experience in these areas? **(Y)** N

(3) Develop your Federal Resume

Did you identify keywords/headlines/themes? **(Y)** N

Did you integrate those into your resume? **(Y)** N

Did you optimize the Additional Information section? **(Y)** N

Did you edit your resume and check character counts? **(Y)** N

(4) Develop Knowledge, Skills and Abilities (KSA) Statements

Does the job require KSA essays or mini-KSAs? **(Y)** N

Did you write them? **(Y)** N

(5) & (6) Apply for the Job, Follow Up, and Interview Prep

Did you read the job again from top to bottom? **(Y)** N

Did you review the closing date, how to apply, and required documents? **(Y)** N

Did you Post Your Resume on USAJOBS.gov? **(Y)** N

Did you complete the Occupational Questionnaire? **(Y)** N

Write the date you applied & the job title and #
May 2, 2018

DHS, Legislative Affairs, Job No. 339-DHS-59917

Did you receive written and/or verbal confirmation? Y N

Have you prepared for the interview? Y N

Did you follow up after two, four, and/or eight weeks? Y N

Write down dates of follow up: _____

_____

CareerPro Global, Inc. | (800) 471-9201 | www.careerproplus.com | www.militaryresumewriters.com

Checkpoint Notes

Checkpoint Notes

Checkpoint 6

Prepare for the Interview

PREPARE FOR THE INTERVIEW

STEPS FOR INTERVIEW PREP

So, you got the call, and they want to bring you in for the interview. Great! But now what?

There are countless websites, articles, and resources out there about interviewing, and many of them share valuable information. In this checkpoint, we'll attempt to distill some of the proven best practices into a clear and concise process you can review each time you interview.

A week or more before the set interview date:

1. Review the Job Announcement and your application materials. Make sure you are familiar with the job. Think about the reasons you applied for the position, and the ways that you demonstrated your qualifications in your resume.

2. Research the organization's website/media presence/current events. Spend maybe half an hour conducting research on the organization so you have a feel for what it's been engaged in recently, along with current and future priorities. This will help to broaden your knowledge and perspective, and become clear on what you can bring to the table, on where you might fit in to the mission.

In today's information economy, background information is available for every company or organization that might be a prospective employer. Research is a critical component of your interview warm-up.

You should be prepared to spend a few hours learning how to research a company. Start with a Google search and see where it leads. Read the company website. Check social media pages, posts, and recommendations. Look for recent announcements and news about the company. You'll want to get a good overview of the company's products, services, and their brand reputation, but you'll also be looking for details and clues about their culture, leadership, and current initiatives.

Your goal is to gain enough understanding of the organization's operations, products, people, and objectives to see how you might fit into the scheme of things. You'll also want to know as much as you can about their expectations of the person who will fill the open slot.

If you have a sense of specific ways that you can contribute, you'll be able to tailor your interview responses and the conversation toward the topic that really matters—how you can make a positive impact for your prospective employer.

Here are a few places you can dig in for the details:

EDGAR: Annual reports are a great source of company information, but they're not included on every company website. The Security and Exchange Commission's (SEC) EDGAR database will let you look up annual and quarterly reports for any publicly traded company.

The reports use a standard format, and you'll want to look for the Management Discussion and Analysis section for information about company initiatives, new product launches, and sector performance.

LinkedIn: Company pages on LinkedIn may provide some valuable insights, but the better use of the business social network is as a resource for direct contacts within a company. Use the search feature to search by company name, then move to the "People" tab to see employees who are active on LinkedIn.

you'll need to wear your skeptic's hat. Reviews, especially from former employees, trend toward the negative.

3. Rehearse CCAR examples and professional summary. Spend maybe an hour rehearsing three to five CCAR examples that demonstrate your abilities to perform the job.

There's no way to know exactly what they might ask, but quite often, they will want to discuss behavioral-based situations and how you have, or would have, handled them in the past.

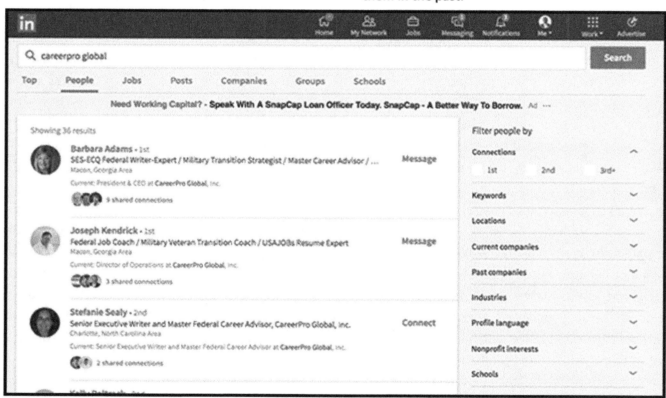

Check your network and ask for introductions, or try to make direct contact with a few people within the company who may be able to give you some insight about the company and the job in which you're interested.

Glassdoor.com: Glassdoor features company reviews and sample interview questions for many larger companies. It's a fascinating site, and you'll find some interesting information from current and former employees, but

By thinking through a few examples, you won't be caught off guard. Likewise, almost every interview includes a question along the lines of "Why do you think we should hire you? Why are you the best fit? What makes you unique?" It's best to rehearse the kinds of things you might say here, and the professional summary in your resume can serve as a good guide; however, we don't recommend trying to memorize a "script."

4. Select your clothing the week before the interview. You'll want to dress at least in business casual, and we recommend selecting and cleaning/preparing your desired outfit a week early. This seems like a minor thing, but it helps to minimize last-minute delays or stress on the day of the interview.

5. Final preparation. The night before the interview, spend maybe 30 minutes briefly reviewing your materials and potential CCAR stories again. How do you practice for a job interview? It's more than just thinking about what might take place. When musicians warm up, the exercise involves the musical instrument and produces some noise. So should your interview be a warm-up!

Here are several tips for your interview practice routine:

- Know the answers to the standard questions: Glassdoor has put together a list of "50 Most Common Interview Questions." Read them, formulate, your answers, and practice the answers out loud: https://www.glassdoor.com/blog/common-interview-questions/

- Anticipate other questions you might hear. In specific, think about behavior-based interview questions that you might be asked. These are experiential questions that an increasing number of large employers and government agencies are using. Behavior-based interviews work on the assumption that past experience indicates future behavior. You'll be asked to provide experiences and examples of actions you have taken that produced results. It's best to prepare these stories ahead of time and practice the way you respond.

- Prepare a list of questions you'd like to ask: What do you want to know about the company? What information would you like to fill in after your research? You'll be judged by both your answers and your questions.

- Get verbal: Practice in front of a mirror or find a friend to role play with you. You might also want to record your practice to see how you sound. This advice may sound obsessive, but actors know that there's a real difference between memorizing the lines and saying them out loud.

- Get visual: Prepare for both phone and video interviews. Many employers and recruiters prefer to use Skype and other networks for initial interviews and for subsequent interviews if those involved are dispersed in many locations. Choose the location. Interview in your office or a more formal setting, but not at the kitchen table. Your appearance, eye contact, and your ability to connect are just as important on an online connection as in person (even if you're barefoot and wearing pajama bottoms underneath the desk).

- Get your act together: Allow enough time for final preparations before the interview. Fix your hair, dress appropriately, and be 10 minutes early. Bring a copy of your resume and a pad or portfolio for notes. Turn off your cell phone! Better yet, leave it in the glove compartment of your car.

Once you've practiced and prepared, it's time to give yourself a break and "let it go" a little bit. We recommend that you plan a relaxing evening, whether that means a quiet dinner at home, walking the dog, or enjoying a movie night.

Doing something that feels "normal" will further help to reduce stress and keep you from overanalyzing the "what-if" questions we all tend to get stuck on before an interview—e.g., "What if they don't like me? What if they ask me something I don't know?"

6. Get a good night's sleep. The night before, do your best to get at least seven hours of sleep. If you can, it's a great idea to do some morning exercise followed by a light breakfast. This will help reduce the stomach jitters. In the final hours before the interview, our best advice is to do something that will help you to RELAX! Maybe sit at a park or a quiet coffee shop for a few minutes. Listen to some music. You've done your best, you've prepared, you know you're qualified, and now it's up to the hiring agency.

7. Be yourself. When you walk through the door, it's time to smile and be as enthusiastic and professional as possible. They don't want to hire some unrealistic or unnatural version of you. They'll be working with you directly, so this is a chance for them to get to know you a little. So just have an open mind, take a couple of moments/breaths before answering, and most importantly, be yourself! You've done amazing things so far, and if they hire you, they'll get to see your unlimited potential firsthand!

Susan's Story and Worksheet

This is where Susan's story and worksheet both come to an end. She is prepared for her interview and confident that her resume will stand out and represent her strongly. There are many unknown variables to the federal hiring process such as competition, internal candidates, and subjective reviewers. Susan knows this, but she also knows that she has done her very best to prepare! Turn the page to see what her worksheet would look like.

CareerPro Global
YOUR CAREER IS OUR BUSINESS®

Roadmap to Federal Jobs Worksheet

Instructions: This worksheet is designed to use each time you apply for a federal job. It's best to follow the checkpoints in order, and don't move on until you complete all the steps in a given checkpoint. Once you apply for a job and begin preparing for the interview, simply go back to checkpoint 1 and start again with your next application. Cast a wide net and follow the best practices in the book, and you should eventually find the perfect federal job for you! And remember, you can always refer back to the Roadmap to Federal Jobs book for more detailed information in each area.

Check Point 1 — Select a Starting Point

List Federal Agencies and Jobs of Interest:

Department of Homeland Security

U.S. Agency for International Development

Legislative Affairs

Public Affairs

Check Point 2 — Determine Your Qualifications for a Specific Job

Write the Job Title/Agency _DHS, Legislative Affairs,_
Job No. 339-DHS-59917

Did you review the duties? (Y) N

Will you be able to show your experience/abilities in your resume? (Y) N

Did you review the special qualifications and/or KSAs? (Y) N

Will you be able to demonstrate your experience in these areas? (Y) N

Check Point 3 — Develop your Federal Resume

Did you identify keywords/headlines/themes? (Y) N

Did you integrate those into your resume? (Y) N

Did you optimize the Additional Information section?
(Y) N

Did you edit your resume and check character counts?
(Y) N

Check Point 4 — Develop Knowledge, Skills and Abilities (KSA) Statements

Does the job require KSA essays or mini-KSAs? (Y) N

Did you write them? (Y) N

Check Point 5 & 6 — Apply for the Job, Follow Up, and Interview Prep

Did you read the job again from top to bottom? (Y) N

Did you review the closing date, how to apply, and required documents? (Y) N

Did you Post Your Resume on USAJOBS.gov? (Y) N

Did you complete the Occupational Questionnaire? (Y) N

Write the date you applied & the job title and #

May 2, 2018

DHS, Legislative Affairs, Job No. 339-DHS-59917

Did you receive written and/or verbal confirmation? (Y) N

Have you prepared for the interview? (Y) N

Did you follow up after two, four, and/or eight weeks?(Y) N

Write down dates of follow up: _____

May 16, 30, June 13, 27

CareerPro Global, Inc. | (800) 471-9201 | www.careerproplus.com | www.militaryresumewriters.com

Checkpoint Notes

_____

_____

_____

_____

_____

_____

_____

_____

_____

_____

_____

_____

_____

Checkpoint Notes

Checkpoint 7

Special Guidance for Military Personnel, Veterans, and Spouses

Check Point 7

SPECIAL GUIDANCE FOR MILITARY PERSONNEL, VETERANS, AND SPOUSES

LEVERAGING MILITARY EXPERIENCE

If you are a veteran, or still on Active Duty or in the Reserve, you may want to consider entering the federal workforce. You would still follow the same steps in this book, but the process of developing your resume may require a bit more finesse to "translate" your military experience into language that civilian hiring managers can understand and appreciate.

If you've served in the military and want to find a federal government job, FedsHireVets.gov provides information on Veterans' Preference, special hiring authorities, and other tips for veterans and transitioning service members seeking federal civilian jobs.

There are also numerous resources available to help members of the active military transition to post-military life, such as the Veterans' Employment & Training Service (VETS) and Transition Assistance Program (TAP).

Still, some of the biggest challenges associated with helping former Active Duty members transition include identifying where their unique skill sets and talents would be a fit within the federal landscape.

The good news is that the U.S. military provides a wealth of training, education, and opportunity that can transition to the federal landscape.

For example, those with government clearance levels (Secret or Top Secret) are typically among the highest sought-after professionals in good-paying jobs involving technology, finance, and planning.

Likewise, specialized skills acquired in the military, such as Air Traffic Control or mechanical repair of vehicles and aircraft, can often be transferred to the federal government and, in fact, help a candidate land a position at a higher-grade level and/or step, depending on the job requirements and the need for any additional training.

The bottom line is that numerous niche markets within the federal government would welcome the skills and accomplishments a transitioning veteran has to offer.

These include maintenance, Information Technology (IT), Information Assurance (IA), aviation, operations, logistics, transportation, finance, security, intelligence operations, medical, legal, training, and general management.

Translating Military Skills

There are several tools to help you translate military skills into federal employment.

One such tool can be found at www.military.com/skills-translator/mos-translator, which allows a person to input his/her Military Occupational Specialty (MOS) number or job title and military branch and then conduct a search that will provide a list with equivalent civilian occupations, many of which have federal equivalents.

On the next page is just a small sampling of some various MOS positions and their possible federal equivalents.

MOS/Position	Possible Federal Equivalent
Signal Officer	Communications Project Manager
Non-Commissioned Officer	Trainer/Team Leader
Commissioned Officer	Project or Program Manager
Military Police	Law Enforcement Officer/Security
Cargo/Supply Specialist	Logistics Specialist
Human Intelligence Collector	Intelligence Analyst
Dental Specialist	Dental Assistant
Healthcare Specialist	Hospital Staff
Journalist	Reporter/Journalist
Administrative Specialist	Human Resources/Office Assistant

Below is a sample list of various MOS/positions and their related skills:

MOS/Position	Related Skills
Signal Officer	Management, Planning, Communications Planning, Satellite Communications
Non-Commissioned Officer	Training, Counseling, Small Group Instruction, Leadership
Commissioned Officer	Project Management, Advising, Strategic Planning, Team Building, Leadership
Military Police	Law Enforcement, Security Operations, Weapons Training, Self-Defense
Cargo/Supply Specialist	Logistics Planning, Supply Management, Inventory, Inspection, Acquisition, Procurement
Human Intelligence Collector	Intelligence Analysis/Collection, Advising
Infantry Team Leader	Small Group Leadership, Training, Planning, Land Navigation, Weapons Proficiency
Dental Specialist	Dental Operations/Administration
Healthcare Specialist	Hospital Patient Care Operations/Administration, Patient Assessment, Basic
Journalist	Reporting, Writing, Researching, Interviewing, Media Escort
Administrative Specialist	Human Resources, Recordkeeping, Data Entry, Word Processing, Scheduling

Let's say that you were a Supply Specialist serving in the Army. Based on the areas of expertise acquired, you could be eligible for several positions within the GS-0300 (General Administrative, Clerical, and Office Services Group), including Mail and Files (0305), Work Unit Supervising (0313), Administrative Officer (0341), Support Services (0342), Management and Program Analyst (0343), Management and Program Clerical and Assistance (0344), Logistics Management (0346), and Equipment Operator (0350).

When searching for clues in your military background, you might want to review the following documentation:

• VMET (Verification of Military Experience and Training)
• DD-214 (record of separation)
• Awards
• Recommendations
• Performance Appraisals
• College Transcripts
• Official Orders

Another excellent resource to help transitioning military clients is the O*NET Military Crosswalk Search at http://www.online.onetcenter.org/crosswalk/MOC.

This useful tool, provided by the U.S. Department of Labor, has thousands of listings for the various military branches and their related Occupational Specialties.

Identifying Pay Scales

Another challenge for military personnel transitioning to the federal government is identifying what pay level they should target.

Below you'll find a loose outline of how to classify where you might fall on the federal pay scale. As always, we recommend that you review the announcement carefully to ensure you can provide sufficient evidence supporting your eligibility for a specific pay level. We also recommend visiting the U.S. Office of Personnel Management

(OPM) at http://www.opm.gov/fedclass/html/gsfunctn.asp, where you can download functional guides (in PDF format) of the various Occupational Specialties, many of which explain what qualifications, knowledge, skills, and abilities a candidate needs to have in order to be eligible for a specific pay level.

GS Pay Level	Military Equivalents
1-4	Enlisted (E-1 to E-4)
5-6	Non-Commissioned Officer (E-5 to E-6)/Staff Non-Commissioned Officer (E-7 through E-9)
7-11	Company Grade Officer (O-1 to O-3) and W-1 to W-4
12-15	Field Grade Officer (O-4 to O-6)
SES	General/Flag Officer (O-7 to O-10)

If your client is on the "cusp" of a particular pay scale, it's always better to apply for the lower level. Because the federal government has a structured employee evaluation program, many times, a professional can achieve salary increases and merit promotions much more quickly than h/she might achieve in the private sector.

Veterans' Preference and Hiring Authorities

The federal government also provided special hiring preference to those who have served. Specifically, veterans can receive "points" that can make them more competitive, since they may receive preference over non-veteran applicants in the hiring process. You should determine your own status by visiting this Department of Labor website (https://webapps.dol.gov/elaws/vets/vetpref/mservice.htm), but Veterans' Preference is normally awarded as follows:

- 5-point preference is the preference granted to a preference-eligible veteran who does not meet the criteria for one of the types of 10-point preferences.

- 10-point (disability) preference is the preference to which a disabled veteran is entitled.

- 10-point (compensable disability) preference is the preference to which a disabled veteran is entitled if h/she has a compensable service-connected disability rating of 10% or more.

- 10-point (30% compensable disability) preference is the preference to which a disabled veteran is entitled if h/she is entitled to a 10-point preference due to a compensable service-connected disability of 30% or more.

- 10-point (other) preference is the preference granted to the widow/widower or mother of a deceased veteran or to the spouse or mother of a disabled veteran. This is also known as "derived preference" because it is derived from the military service of someone else— a veteran who is not using it for personal preference.

Veterans may also be eligible for one of the special hiring authorities below, and can learn more at this link: https://www.fedshirevets.gov/job/shav/

- Veterans Recruitment Appointment (VRA)
- 30% or More Disabled Veteran
- Veterans Employment Opportunity Act of 1998 (VEOA)
- Disabled Veterans Enrolled in a VA Training Program
- Schedule A Appointing Authority: Agencies can use this hiring authority to appoint eligible veterans who

have a severe physical, psychological, or intellectual disability.

Veterans Program Offices

In 2009, the President issued Executive Order 13518 (Veterans Employment Initiative), which mandated the creation of Veterans Employment Program Offices.

These offices are responsible for promoting veterans' recruitment, employment, training and development, and retention within their respective agencies.

We encourage you to contact these offices, listed below, for specific information about employment opportunities in these agencies.

AGENCY	PHONE
Agency for International Development	(202) 712-5663
Department of Agriculture	(202) 690-3420
Department of Commerce	(202) 482-4270
Department of Defense	(888) 363-4872
Department of Education	(202) 401-3855
Department of Energy	(202) 586-5880
Department of Health and Human Services	(202) 260-6117
Department of Homeland Security	(202) 357-8620
Department of Housing and Urban Development	(202) 402-2018
Department of the Interior	(877) 227-1969
Department of Justice	(202) 514-0349
Department of Labor	(202) 693-0260
Department of State	(202) 663-2182
Department of the Treasury	(202) 927-VETS
Department of Transportation	(202) 366-1779
Department of Transportation, Federal Aviation Administration	(501) 918-4415
Department of Veterans Affairs	(866) 606-6206
Environmental Protection Agency	(202) 564-5233
General Services Administration	(202) 694-8137
National Aeronautics and Space Administration	(202) 358-1297
National Science Foundation	(703) 292-7893
Nuclear Regulatory Commission	(301) 415-7400
Office of Personnel Management	(202) 606-2825
Small Business Administration	(303) 844-7787

Military Spouse Programs

There are also many wonderful opportunities for military spouses and family members to secure employment within the federal government. USAJOBS has some fantastic guidance on its website for military spouses, and has even created an easy-to-spot icon to alert you if a particular job will consider spouse preference.

How do I know a job is open to military spouses?	In the job announcement look for the **This job is open to** section. When a job is open to **Military Spouses** you'll see this icon: ⬤ There may be other groups listed that can also apply.
	You can also select the **Military spouses** filter in search. Your results will display all jobs open to military spouses.

Military Spouse Appointing Authority (Executive Order 13473)

This allows agencies to appoint a military spouse without competition. Agencies can choose to use this authority when filling Competitive Service positions on a temporary (not to exceed 1 year), term (more than 1 year but not more than 4 years), or permanent basis.

As a military spouse, you are eligible under this authority if your Active Duty military spouse: 1) receives a Permanent Change of Station (PCS) move; 2) has a 100% disability rating; or 3) died while on Active Duty. Each of these categories has different eligibility criteria that must be met.

Military Spouse Preference Program (Program S)

As part of the Department of Defense Priority Placement Program (PPP), Program S provides employment preference for spouses of Active Duty military members.
Learn more here: https://www.cpms.osd.mil/Content/Documents/PPP-Program%20S.pdf

Derived Spouse Preference

Derived Preference is a method in which the spouse, widow/widower, or mother of a veteran may be eligible to claim Veterans' Preference when the veteran is unable to use it. You can be given "XP" Preference in appointment

if you meet the eligibility criteria. Both a mother and a spouse (including widow or widower) may be entitled to preference based on the same veteran's service if they both meet the requirements. However, neither may receive preference if the veteran is living and is qualified for federal employment.

Spouse of Relocating Military Member or DOD Civilian - Appointable

Applicants who are spouses of relocating Active Duty military members or Department of Defense (DOD) civilian employees may apply to job announcements regardless of information listed under the "Who May Apply" section during the 30 days preceding through the six months following their sponsor's relocation to the activity's commuting area.

Overseas Military Spouse Appointment

You may be eligible for this hiring category if you are the spouse of an Active Duty U.S. Armed Forces service member who meets the following conditions:

- You and the sponsor were married prior to the relocation (before the PCS); and
- Since the relocation, you have not accepted or declined a permanent position or a temporary position of one year or longer at the new duty station of the sponsor; and
- You are among the Best Qualified; and

- The position applied for is not above the highest permanent grade previously held in the Federal Service.

This preference can be granted only once per PCS relocation, and once you accept or decline a continuing position (one that is expected to last one year or more), your eligibility for preference terminates, regardless of whether preference was applied.

Overseas Family Member Preference

You may be eligible for this hiring category if you are the spouse or unmarried dependent child (including stepchild, adopted child, and foster child) not more than 23 years of age who:

- Resides with a member of the U.S. Armed Forces or a U.S. citizen employee of a U.S. government agency (including NAF activities) whose duty station is in the foreign area; **AND**

- Has not accepted or declined a permanent position or a temporary position of one year or longer at the new duty station of the sponsor.

This preference does not apply to family members of locally hired civilian employees.

Checkpoint Notes

Checkpoint 8

The Senior Executive Service (SES)

Check Point 8

THE SENIOR EXECUTIVE SERVICE (SES)

WHAT IS THE SES?

Up until now, we have primarily focused on federal employees who qualify for any position ranked GS-1 through GS-15. However, there is another level of federal employees that, when compared to the civilian workforce, would be the equivalent of senior leaders—the SES (Senior Executive Service).

Founded as part of the Civil Service Reform Act of 1978, the SES is comprised of the men and women charged with leading the continuing transformation of government. These leaders possess well-honed executive skills and share a broad perspective of government and a public service commitment.

Members of the SES serve in the key positions just below the top Presidential appointees (e.g., the Presidential Cabinet), and represent the major link between these appointees and the rest of the federal workforce. Since the SES is the highest competitive level a candidate can reach in the federal government, it's a very competitive program because there are only a few positions within each agency.

Within the SES, there are two subcategories, as follows:

- **ST** (Scientific and Professional) positions are classified above the GS-15 level and involve high-level research and development. ST positions are established under 5 USC 3104 and are always in the Competitive Service.

- **SL** (Senior-Level) positions are classified above GS-15. The work of the position does not involve the fundamental Research and Development responsibilities that are characteristic of ST positions. SL positions may

be in either the Competitive or the Excepted Service. The vast majority of SES positions are SL positions.

Executive Core Qualifications (ECQs)

All SES candidates must be able to demonstrate a high level of proficiency in all five ECQs below:

1. Leading Change—The ability to bring about strategic change, both within and outside the organization, to meet organizational goals. Inherent to this ECQ is the ability to establish an organizational vision and to implement it in a continually changing environment. Characteristics that should be demonstrated in this ECQ include Creativity and Innovation, External Awareness, Flexibility, Resilience, Strategic Thinking, and Vision.

2. Leading People—The ability to lead people toward meeting the organization's vision, mission, and goals. Inherent to this ECQ is the ability to provide an inclusive workplace that fosters the development of others, facilitates cooperation and teamwork, and supports constructive resolution of conflicts. Characteristics that should be demonstrated in this ECQ include Conflict Management, Leveraging Diversity, Developing Others, and Team Building.

3. Results Driven—The ability to meet organizational

goals and customer expectations. Inherent to this ECQ is the ability to make decisions that produce high-quality results by applying technical knowledge, analyzing problems, and calculating risks. Characteristics that should be demonstrated in this ECQ include Accountability, Customer Service, Decisiveness, Entrepreneurship, Problem Solving, and Technical Credibility.

4. Business Acumen—The ability to manage human, financial, and information resources strategically. Characteristics that should be demonstrated in this ECQ include Financial Management, Human Capital Management, and Technology Management.

5. Building Coalitions—The ability to build coalitions internally and with other federal agencies, state and local governments, non-profit and private-sector organizations, foreign governments, or international organizations to achieve common goals. Characteristics that should be demonstrated in this ECQ include Partnering, Political Savvy, and Influencing/Negotiating.

How Does SES Differ from the General Schedule?

Some primary differences between SES and the General Schedule (GS) positions include:

- Veterans do not receive hiring preference for SES positions; this is because 5 USC 2108(3), which defines the term "preference eligible," states that this term does not include applicants for, or members of, the SES.

- SES members have their own association: The Senior Executive Association (SEA). The SEA is a professional association representing the interests of the members of the career SES. SEA maintains a website on which members may access valuable resources, including legal help and member forums.

- SES members do not necessarily have to be status candidates. In an effort to recruit the best and brightest leaders, more and more agencies are opening up their SES candidate pool to people from the private industry who are able to exhibit the ECQs within a context that would fit the open SES position.

Determining Your Eligibility for SES

Many people transitioning to the federal government are often attracted to the high level of responsibility and compensation offered at the SES level. However, just because someone has run his/her own small business and held the title of CEO or CIO doesn't necessarily mean that h/she is automatically eligible for SES status.

Eligibility falls into one of three categories, as follows:

Criterion A cases are based on demonstrated executive experience. Candidates must demonstrate that they have experience/competence in all five ECQs as part of their application for SES positions.

Criterion B cases are based on successful participation in an OPM-approved SES Candidate Development Program (CDP). Candidates who compete government-wide and successfully complete a CDP are eligible for non-competitive appointment to the SES. However, successful completion does not guarantee placement in the SES.

Criterion C cases are based on the candidates having special or unique qualities that indicate a likelihood of success in the SES. Candidates must demonstrate that they have the qualifications for the position and the potential to quickly acquire full competence in the five ECQs.

The package submitted for Qualifications Review Board (QRB) approval must contain the agency's assessment of why the selectee uniquely qualifies for the position and an Individual Development Plan (IDP) that focuses on the specific ECQs that need to be enhanced.

The SES Application Process

The SES application process is highly competitive and can be quite daunting and intimidating for some applicants. The vacancy announcements, which are posted on USA-JOBS.gov , require a resume, and normally 10-20 or more pages or executive and technical essays.

However, the process can be successfully negotiated by presenting your most valuable contributions and potential assets to the hiring organization through robust, descriptive, and compelling language.

First, you need a resume that clearly demonstrates your progressive leadership and potential over the past 10 years. Avoid using a "laundry list" of your basic job duties, and instead try to show executive scope, impact, and results.

Since at least 2014, the standard for SES resumes is a five-page format with size 12 font and 1" margins all around. However, you should check each vacancy announcement for specific application instructions, and ask the HR contact if you need clarification.

The agency has the option of including Technical Qualifications, or TQs (they usually do), which drill down into some of the specific "technical" areas you will be expected to oversee in the position.

 CPG Exclusive

If your client applied with the new, five-page, "all-inclusive resume format," h/she may be asked (depending on the agency) to provide expanded ECQs at this time.

Again, it's best to use the CCAR format and stick to size 12 font with 1" margins. Each TQ is a different, but it usually works great to provide a brief "introductory" response/ paragraph to the question, followed by one or two specific examples in the CCAR format.

The SES process is as follows:

1) Application is received and reviewed by lower-level HR specialists to ensure all materials asked for in the vacancy announcement are included with the application and that all instructions were followed. Those who make this "cut" will then be passed to mid-level HR specialists who will check the application for "minimum qualifications."

2) Those applications making it past the first two screenings may be referred to the hiring agency's Executive Review Board (ERB) to review all applications. This is the point where the Technical Qualification (TQs) are critical. Failure to meet any one of the mandatory technical or executive core qualification standards will eliminate a candidate from further consideration.

3) A screening panel composed of a diverse mix of senior executives will evaluate candidates. The panel members will individually review each of the applications in terms of the qualifications criteria contained in the announcement.

The panel will reach a consensus decision as to the "Best Qualified," "Qualified," or "Not Qualified" candidates. Each application will be given a score between 70 and 100 and only those applicants who score in the top 10% based upon the entire application are considered viable candidates.

4) The panel will interview the top 10% of the "Best Qualified" candidates based upon consistently applied criteria. The panel will then make a recommendation of those who should be referred to the selecting official, in priority order.

If there is any debate, discussion, or disagreement about who the selected candidate will be, the scores of each of the candidates' TQs will be used to "break the tie." Final selection of a candidate is contingent upon the selecting authority.

After the interviews, several names will be referred to the Selecting Official, then sent to the hiring agency, and then to OPM for vetting.

Some agencies will then have their high-level HR (or in some cases, hired consultants) thoroughly review your ECQs and put you through a "mock review board" to give feedback and input before sending to OPM for certification.

Finally, a job offer is made, and the selected candidate's ECQs are sent up to OPM for certification (or not) by a QRB.

If OPM does not consider the applicant to be "SES material" (based upon breadth and scope of answers to ECQs), the applicant is rejected and the agency is notified.

If OPM finds that the applicant has not adequately addressed the 28 required core competencies, OPM will send the ECQs back to the agency and the applicant is usually given some limited timeframe to correct deficiencies and then resubmit.

If OPM considered the ECQs to be demonstrative of Executive Core Qualifications, they will be certified by OPM and the applicant will never have to generate another set of ECQs again.

Why ECQs Get Disapproved

The QRB members will be representative of any of the 200-plus government agencies. They will not necessarily be familiar with your background or specialty area, so it's important to state your accomplishments in clear, non-technical language that any executive can understand. ECQs must tell a narrative, engaging story of your client's impact in executive leadership terms in a business/corporate environment.

Over the years, we have assisted thousands of people with applying for SES positions. However, some people decide to write their own ECQs, and some of them turn to us for help when they get disqualified and the QRB calls for a rewrite. In these cases, the QRB provides feedback as to why they rejected the ECQs. The following excerpts will demonstrate how stringent and specific the QRBs tend to be:

"...did not present evidence of, or demonstrate, executive leadership in the write-up. Accomplishments appeared to be routine staff work. There appeared to be no substantial challenges as well as no significant results that had impact on the organization."

"The QRB noted that the candidate's ECQ statement was weak and lacked scope and depth, and did not delve into experiences that demonstrate executive leadership. Overall the QRB noted that it was difficult to determine if the candidate possesses the leadership and executive level qualifications. Board noted that accomplishments

appeared more on a manager's level versus executive. Not enough evidence of executive leadership. Candidate did not appear to have the broad-spectrum focus, rather a narrow and limited focus on the smaller tasks and projects accomplished. Appeared more process-oriented versus outcome-oriented. What difference did the candidate make?"

The chart below outlines the best practices for developing ECQs:

CareerPro Global
YOUR CAREER IS OUR BUSINESS™

How To Write Executive Core Qualifications (ECQs) That the Review Boards Will Love!

CareerPro Global's writers and coaches have developed and refined these best practices while helping over 3,000 corporate, federal, and military leaders apply for Senior Executive Service (SES) positions

Use the 10-year rule: If an example happened more than 10 years ago, don't bother. The board won't like it.

Use the Challenge-Context-Actions-Results (CCAR) format: There are numerous ways to tell a story, but the Office of Personnel Management (OPM) wants your career stories presented in a logical format on the page, using Challenge-Context-Actions-Results. In addition, examples should include specific, impactful results.

Present executive narratives, not project management descriptions: It is easy to share detailed, technical write-ups of projects, but OPM wants specific career stories that are impactful and executive in scope. For instance, did you work with senior officials, cross organizational lines, and create results that have widespread and long-term strategic impact? It is also best to keep the reader in mind, and assume that they do not share your background. Simply put: express stories in a clear, concise way that any executive can understand and appreciate.

Use two examples per ECQ: OPM will accept one example per ECQ, but it is strongly recommended that you provide two each. Here is another tip: For ECQ#4, Business Acumen, think of it as three separate "mini-ECQs." The whole write up still needs to fit within two pages, but it is best to present one strong CCAR example for each of the following areas – Financial, Technology, and Human Capital Management.

Use the competencies as your guide: Don't overlook the critical importance of telling your career stories through the "lens" of the competencies. Instead, use the process below as a powerful decision making tool.

1 BRAINSTORM
With all of these best practices in mind, take the time to write down two potential topics for each ECQ (three for Business Acumen).

2 OUTLINE/COMPARE
Before you write your ECQs, you should outline your potential topics and then compare them to the competencies for each ECQ. Next, ask yourself, "Will I be able to address most, if not all, of these competencies effectively in my write-up?" If the answer is yes, you are probably on the right track. However, if the answer is no, or if it is unclear, then your topic may not be a good fit for that particular ECQ. The boards will be looking for evidence of the competencies in your ECQs.

3 DEVELOP
Once you have considered all of the best practices, and completed step one and two, you are ready to develop your ECQs!

ECQs & the Competencies

Leading Change	Leading People	Results Driven	Business Acumen	Building Coalitions
Creativity /Innovation	Conflict Mgmt	Accountability	Financial Mgmt	Partnering
External Awareness	Leveraging Diversity	Customer Service	Human Capital Mgmt	Political Savvy
Flexibility	Developing Others	Decisiveness	Technology Mgmt	Influencing and/or
Resilience	Team Building	Entrepreneurship		Negotiating
Strategic Thinking		Problem Solving		
Vision		Technical Credibility		

Fundamental Competencies
No need to address fundamental competencies directly, but they should be addressed over the course of the complete ECQ narrative...

Interpersonal Skills	Written Communication	Oral Communication	Continual Learning	Integrity & Honesty	Public Service Motivation

Candidate Development Program (CDP)

If you are determined to gain employment in the SES, but don't yet have the necessary qualifications, you may be interested in a government-offered CDP designed to help give candidates a competitive edge for SES consideration.

Participating agencies that offer an SES CDP have collaborated with trainers to ensure candidates receive the most comprehensive training to prepare them for a challenging career at the SES level.

The CDP class size typically consists of 20-50 eligible participants who are at the GS-14 or -15 level, and have put in at least one year's time in that grade.

While the class size, application process, and topics vary according to the agency, typically, the program must be completed within 12-18 months of enrollment and concurrently with a candidate fulfilling his/her other job responsibilities.

The goal of a CDP is to:

1) Prepare participants for SES certification by OPM
2) Establish a pool of qualified candidates for SES positions
3) Prepare future executives for collaborative leadership

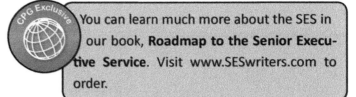

You can learn much more about the SES in our book, **Roadmap to the Senior Executive Service**. Visit www.SESwriters.com to order.

Activities of the CDP include a combination of lectures, workshops, seminars, guest speakers, group meetings, and field trips, as well as:

- Leadership development experiences
- Personal skills and behavioral assessment
- Leadership training
- Capitol Hill exposure
- Developmental assignments
- Action learning projects
- Mentoring
- Team-building exercises

The program also features feedback-intensive and mentoring components to further assist candidates in their developmental journey. Candidates who complete the program and obtain certification by an SES QRB may be selected for an SES position anywhere in the federal government without further competition.

Additional information about the SES application process can be found at http://www.opm.gov/ses/references/GuidetoSESQuals_2010.pdf.

Checkpoint Notes

Federal Career Toolbox

Resume Samples Using Our Signature Headline Format

Table of Contents

PRIVATE SECTOR TO WG-12: AIRCRAFT MECHANIC

> This client was seeking to leverage his automotive and aviation background and move into the government sector to work on a military base.

Joseph L. LaCaze
332 Oleander Circle
Perry, MN 55555 US
Day Phone: 478-333-3333 - Ext:
Email: myname@yahoo.com

Work Experience:
Saturn Aviation
57 Hwy 30 West
Shreveport , LA   81169 United States

03/2016 - Present
Salary: 15.36 USD Per Hour
Hours per week: 40
Lead Sheet Metal and Composite Mechanic

Duties, Accomplishments and Related Skills:
AIRCRAFT SUPPORT OPERATIONS: Fabricate, repair, and install a variety of sheet metal components and equipment for Boeing 777, Embraer, Gulfstream, and Global Hawk aircraft. Produce and repair sheet metal and composite aircraft engine cowling, spoilers, ailerons, elevators, rudders, flight control surfaces, and components for composite fuselage structures. Reference technical orders (TOs), manufacturer's specifications, engineering orders, schematics, and block diagrams to determine paint, repair, or manufacturing requirements. Maintain inventory levels of parts, materials, tools, and equipment to ensure sufficient levels to support production needs. Actively train, mentor, and evaluate new employees on production procedures and expectations of the company.

PLANNING AND LAYOUT: Interpret blueprints, sketches, drawings, specifications, and work orders to plan and lay out various sheet metal components and structures. Apply basic shop mathematics to calculate and lay out shapes, irregular curves, angles, bend radius, edge distance, and pitch and row spacing and to develop templates and patterns used to lay out work. Employ measuring devices, such as dial calipers, depth gauges, and rulers, to lay out parts. Prepare various components, working with a variety of metals. Mark metal material to indicate cut and bend locations; set up equipment; and cut, shear, and bend each piece according to dimensional specifications. Determine work sequence and select materials, equipment, and tools to be used.

SHEET METAL OPERATIONS: Set up and operate a variety of sheet metal machines to bend and form light-gauge metals into desired shapes, allowing for seams, joints, laps, and shrinkages. Produce components consisting of straight and curved edges with irregular curves and planes. Use various fixtures and holding devices to hold components in place. Join parts by riveting, soldering, and spot welding and install sheet metal sections with bolts, rivets, screws, and other fastening devices. Perform surface preparation by mechanical means, such as scraping, wire brushing, masking, spackling, and sanding, and by chemical methods to remove paint, debris, and corrosion. Clean and prepare parts and structures to ensure adhesion of coating materials.

INSPECTION AND EXAMINATION: Examine and inspect aircraft structures such as frames, stringers, bulk heads, spars, ribs, stiffeners, and trailing and leading edge to locate cracked, punctured, bulged, dented, and broken components and loosened or missing rivets and fasteners. Determine the extent of damage and required repair needed to restore defective components to original strength. Use ultrasonic and/or eddy current equipment to identify, locate, and measure hidden subsurface flaws, corrosion, and separation in bonded honeycomb structures.

QUALITY CONTROL AND PROCESS IMPROVEMENT: Use Lean Manufacturing methodology, Spaghetti diagrams, Time Observation, One-Piece Flow/One-Need Flow, and Pull System to reduce costs and streamline production processes. Apply inspection experience and trade knowledge to interpret test results and make final determinations of parts condition based on TOs and quality standards; tag components as serviceable, repairable, or condemned. Apply ISO 9000/9001 and AS 9100 quality management standards to ensure effective and efficient processes.

SAFETY AND ENVIRONMENTAL PROTECTION: Follow and enforce all Occupational Safety and Health Administration (OSHA) and Environmental Protection Agency (EPA) regulations and guidelines, hazardous waste management rules, shop procedures, and safety and security directives. Use personal protective equipment, including safety shoes, glasses, gloves, and clothing, while performing sheet metal operations and welding procedures. Safely handle, store, and dispose of Hazardous Materials (HAZMAT) and follow Material Safety Data Sheet (MSDS) information. Maintain an orderly and safe working environment using 5S Lean Manufacturing standards. Participate in safety audits and safety meetings to address unsafe conditions and prevention.

TOOLS AND EQUIPMENT: Use precision measuring tools, such as six-inch scale, micrometers, calibers, depth micrometers, protractors, calipers, and height, depth, dial, and screw pitch gauges, and use standard measuring devices such as tape measures and rulers. Operate pan brake, slip roll, crimpers, C-squeezes, punches, hammers, hand slips, chisels, and shrinker/stretcher devices. Operate ground support equipment, including manlifts, scissor lifts, forklifts, and tow trucks.

KEY ACCOMPLISHMENTS:
*Instrumental in saving more than $120K over a three-year period with the redesign of the shop floor and use of a newly developed cell system.
*Recognized as sheet metal and composite material Subject Matter Expert for a variety of aircraft.
*Selected to serve as a member of the Foreign Object Damage (FOD) Committee.

SelectPrime Automotive
9002 Chevy Highway
Barker, LA   88856 United States

06/2008 - 03/2016
Salary: 12.00 USD Per Hour
Hours per week: 40
Automotive Technician

Duties, Accomplishments and Related Skills:
EQUIPMENT MAINTENANCE AND REPAIR: Overhauled, repaired, and maintained a variety of vehicles and equipment, such as cars, buses, trucks, forklifts, warehouse tractors, and light ground maintenance equipment. Performed inspections and checks and used test reports and instructions to determine the nature and extent of repairs required on engines; transmissions; suspension; steering and braking systems; and related electrical, fuel, hydraulic, wheel, and engine systems and assemblies. Dismantled, adjusted, repaired, reassembled, and performed operational checks on systems and compo-

nents. Tuned and adjusted vehicle components to prescribed operating tolerances.

SUPPORT FUNCTIONS: Performed electrical repairs, installing and repairing electrical wiring of various fixtures and equipment. Applied paints, varnish, stains, and lacquer to various surfaces, such as drywall, block wall, metal doors, wood doors, and aluminum siding. Followed safety procedures and made suggestions to improve existing processes. Welded trailers, weight equipment, and lawn equipment. Also served as Service Writer and Customer Service Representative; maintained a loyal customer base by being upfront and honest with each customer. Maintained record of tasks completed using the work order system.

TOOLS AND EQUIPMENT: Used hand and power tools, including pneumatic wrenches, torque wrenches, hammers, drills, ban saws, screw drivers, sanders, grinders, files, and circular saws. Operated cornice break, box and pan break, slip roll, various sizes of tin snips, and a variety of pneumatic sheers and foot sheers to perform sheet metal fabrication of air-conditioning ducts. Used hoist and set up and used scaffolds, ladders, stands, and other equipment to prepare the worksite. Operated specialized testing equipment, such as compression testers, motor analyzers, test benches, and specialized measuring instruments, such as micrometers, Vernier calipers, and dial indicators. Maintained grounds using tractors, mowers, blowers, trimmers, weed eaters, and edgers; used pressure washer and sandblasting equipment to perform cleaning operations.

KEY ACCOMPLISHMENTS:
*Provided outstanding service for more than 600 vehicles, with a flawless safety record.
*Increased customer base by more than five each month due to recommendations from existing clientele.

Education:
Central Maine Technical College Draft, ME United States
Technical or Occupational Certificate 06/2015

Credits Earned: 32
Major: Aircraft Structural Technology

Job Related Training:
Blueprint Reading (8 hours), 11/2017; Composite Part Fabrication (8 hours), 11/2017; Torque Wrench Usage (1 hours), 11/2017; Paint Mixing (6 hours), 10/2017; Overhead Crane and Hoist Operations (5 hours), 09/2017; Application of Cast in Place S (1 hours), 09/2017; Brush Anodizing (3 hours), 08/2017; Sealant Applier (2 hours), 08/2017; Drilling Large Close Tolerance Holes (2 hours), 04/2017; Manufacturing Execution Data System (MEDS) User Production Area (1 hours), 04/2017; Visual Requirements (1 hours), 03/2017; Manufacturing Execution Systems (4 hours), 02/2017; Issue, Use, and Control of Components (2 hours), 02/2017; Foreign Object Damage (FOD) Control (1 hours), 02/2017; Material Handling (2 hours), 02/2017; Working Safety in the Shop (1 hour), 09/2015; Automotive Service Writer Training (8 hours), 02/2006; Fuel Injection System Diagnosis and Service (2 hours), 12/2005; Emission Control Diagnosis and Service (2 hours), 12/2005

Additional Information:

PROFESSIONAL PROFILE:
Motivated, results-oriented professional offering hands-on experience in sheet metal fabrication, equipment maintenance and repair, and customer service. Account for and manage material resources, identifying and mitigating risks and using time efficiently to meet company goals. Demonstrate exceptional ability to independently make judgments and decisions,

applying problem-solving and technical skills to meet demanding schedules. Capable of handling objects weighing up to 20 pounds and occasionally handle objects weighing up to 50 pounds with minimal effort.

RELEVANT AREAS OF EXPERTISE:

SHEET METAL FABRICATION AND ASSEMBLY: Expert in the layout, fabrication, assembly, and installation of sheet metal components and assemblies. Produce components consisting of straight and curved edges with irregular curves and planes. Fabricate and assemble components, such as side and roof panels, body panels, control boxes, instrument clusters, stringers, ribs, stiffeners, and brackets. Join components using various fixtures and holding devices to hold components in place. Fasten seams and joints together with bolts, screws, rivets, specially formed sheet metal drive clips, and welding techniques.

PLANNING AND LAYOUT: Interpret blueprints, sketches, drawings, specifications, and work orders to plan and lay out various sheet metal components and structures. Apply basic shop mathematics to calculate and lay out shapes. Employ measuring devices, such as dial calipers, depth gauges, and rulers, to lay out parts. Prepare various components, working with a variety of metals. Mark metal material to indicate cut and bend locations; set up equipment; and cut, shear, and bend each piece according to dimensional specifications.

SAFETY AND OCCUPATIONAL HEALTH: Work in a manner to prevent damage to tools and materials and avoid injury to others by maintaining sharp hand-eye coordination while performing repetitive actions or operating machines to complete assignments. Follow and enforce all Occupational Safety and Health Administration (OSHA) and Environmental Protection Agency (EPA) regulations and guidelines and company safety and security directives. Use personal protective equipment and follow Material Safety Data Sheet (MSDS) information to safely handle, store, and dispose of Hazardous Materials (HAZMAT).

CUSTOMER SERVICE AND COMMUNICATION SKILLS: Skillful communicator, possessing the ability to effectively relay information and ideas verbally and in writing. Demonstrate exceptional customer-service skills; highly responsive to requests for assistance and support.

COMPUTER SKILLS: Microsoft (MS) Windows Operating Systems; MS Software (Word, Excel, Outlook, and Internet Explorer/Edge); Identifix (shop management system); Mitchell on Demand (online automotive repair information); ALL-DATA Automotive System; Systems Applications and Products (SAP); Manufacturing Execution Data System (MEDS)

PRIVATE SECTOR TO GS-7: DENTAL HYGIENIST

This applicant was seeking a Dental Hygienist position requiring advanced knowledge of oral care, patient treatment plans, patient educational methods, and dental operations management skills.

Maya Sheeler
2222 Arkansas Circle
Smithy, AR 55872 US
Day Phone: 123-456-7890 - Ext:
Email: myname@gmail.com

Work Experience:
Capp City Dental
555 Block Street
Galvanez, MS 44461 United States

12/2013 - Present
Salary: 62,000 USD Per Year
Hours per week: 40
Dental Hygienist

Duties, Accomplishments and Related Skills:
Capp City Dental specializes in general dental health, cosmetic dentistry, and select advanced services such as crowns, dentures, implants, root canal treatments, and bridges.

PATIENT CARE: Use Biolase laser technology products and systems to perform sub gingival debridement and disinfection, and Cavitron ultrasonic system for tartar/plaque removal and tooth surface cleanings. Collaborate with dentists regarding patient treatment plans and specific at-home care. Provide routine oral prophylactic care to include application of fluoride solutions, desensitizing and sealant materials. Make impressions for bleaching and fluoride carrier trays. Adjust and clean patients' removable dental prostheses. Clean calcareous deposits, accretions, and stains from teeth and beneath margins of gums, using dental instruments. Examine gums, using probes, to locate periodontal recessed gums and signs of gum disease. Feel and visually examine gums for sores and signs of disease. Record and review patient medical histories. Chart conditions of decay and disease for diagnosis and treatment by dentist. Apply fluorides or other cavity preventing agents to arrest dental decay. Administer local anesthetic agents. Remove sutures and dressings from oral surgeries. Place and remove rubber dams, matrices, and temporary restorations. Make impressions for study casts.

PATIENT INFORMATION/EDUCATION: Provide clinical services or health education to improve and maintain oral health of patients. Follow up with patients who have had oral surgery or any kind of anesthesia to assess their response and recovery and to answer any questions related to post-operative recovery care. Review patient X-rays and test results and provide clarification or guidance to patients regarding applicable care. Develop patient educational literature for postoperative procedures, preventive care, and other topics related to healthy oral hygiene. Conduct dental health clinics for community groups to augment services of dentist.

REGULATORY COMPLIANCE: Maintain patient confidentiality, per Health Insurance Portability and Accountability Act (HIPAA) regulations. Ensure all patient charts are updated immediately after their treatments conclude and that all records contained accurate information. Ensure proper sterilization and proper maintenance of all dental tools and treatment/oral surgery rooms, per American Dental Association (ADA) and The Joint Commission (formerly the Joint Commission on Accreditation of Healthcare Organizations (JCAHO) regulations. Ensure proper disposal of medical wastes, as per Occupational Safety and Health Administration (OSHA) regulations.

DENTAL OFFICE MANAGEMENT: Use Eaglesoft and Henry Schein Dentrix dental practice management software applications for insurance billing/coding, tracking patient treatment histories, appointment scheduling, accounts receivable, and the management of personalized patient portals. Contact patients by telephone to confirm/schedule appointments and delivered results of dental tests. Relay patient information and messages to staff dentist related to symptoms and medication need. Contact patients' local pharmacies to phone in prescriptions. Manage a control inventory of topical and local anesthetic agents, dental supplies, and tools.

SELECTED ACCOMPLISHMENTS:
*Provided dental support to more than 300 patients.
*Perform digital imaging services using systems such as ScanX Classical Digital Imaging Systems; Spectra Caries Detection Aid; and the Enhanced Oral Assessment System used to detect oral abnormalities.

Bright Star Dental
70 Station Way
Missoula, MT 59812 United States

09/2009 - 11/2013
Salary: 83,000 USD Per Year
Hours per week: 40
Lead, Traditional, and Restorative Hygienist

Duties, Accomplishments and Related Skills:
Bright Star Dental Services is a family practice specializing in the oral hygiene care and restorative treatments of patients of all ages. Specific areas of expertise include preventive/restorative care, cosmetic, endodontics, prosthodontics, and oral surgery.

PATIENT CARE/EXAMS: Took periapical, panoramic, bite wing, and occlusal X-rays to screen for periodontal problems. Reported oral conditions from observations of the patient's mouth, throat, and lymph nodes and glands in neck to the attending dentist. Inspected teeth for plaque, tartar, or grinding. Reassured apprehensive patients by explaining procedures and answering questions. Assisted in the planning and administering of patient treatment plans by interpreting X-rays and other diagnostic reports. Planned dental hygiene procedures for appointments or series of patient appointments. Interviewed patients to obtain medical and dental histories. Advised patients on strategies for plaque control and dietary adjustments.

PREVENTIVE CARE SERVICES: Used ultrasonic devices and hand instruments to remove supra-gingival and subgingival calculus, performed root planing, and applied fluoride and sealants to the teeth; cleaned interproximal surfaces of teeth using dental floss or tape; applied fluoride to the teeth; and performed oral prophylaxis on non-ambulatory patients.

DENTAL HEALTH EDUCATION: Instructed patients in brushing and flossing techniques; caring and removing appliances and bridges, periodontic care, and oral health-related diet and nutrition. Created educational literature, such as flyers, brochures, and information cards, to equip patients with take-home instructions to ensure proper care of dental appliances and/or post-operative treatment. Explained etiology of caries and periodontal diseases to patients; how to perform oral cavity inspections for abnormalities and suspicious lesions; and how to treat common oral issues, such as toothaches, inflamed gums, and minor trauma incurred in the mouth.

ORAL SURGERY: Administered anesthesia and medication, including local anesthesia and topical medications. Desensitized eroded areas of teeth and dispensed non-prescription drugs. Removed sutures and controlled bleeding. Performed gingival curettage and retracted oral tissues during surgery.

ADJUSTMENTS/REPAIRS: Smoothed and polished restorations and removable appliances. Filed sharp edges of fractured teeth. Took teeth impressions for molds used to create dentures.

RESTORATIVE CARE: Performed numerous restorative care procedures including, but not limited to, applying cavity liner/base; placing, carving and finishing amalgam restorations; placing and finishing composite and temporary restorations; placing and/or remove temporary crowns; and adjusting occlusions on amalgams, composite, and temporary restorations.

OFFICE MANAGEMENT: Updated patients charts electronically, prepared insurance claims with proper procedural codes, and scheduled patient appointments and follow-up visits. Prepared all dental instruments by properly sterilizing, storing, and inspecting items prior to future use. Disposed medical wastes and hazardous contaminants, per OSHA regulations. Prepared surgical and treatment suites, instruments, and equipment before and after patient treatments. Managed a comprehensive medical and dental supply inventory that included perishable and non-perishable items.

SELECTED ACCOMPLISHMENTS:
*Provided dental support to more than 450 patients.
*Noted for ability to perform effective patient interviews to obtain symptom information and to gain insight into the patient's and his/her family's medical histories.

Education:
Pacific University Oregon, Forest Grove, OR United States
Bachelor's Degree 06/2012
GPA: 4.0/4.0 Magna cum laude
Credits Earned: 61
Major: Dental Hygiene
Relevant Coursework, Licensures and Certifications:
Transferred course credit from community college programs specific to dental hygiene. Course credit was accepted toward Bachelor of Science degree program

Additional courses accepted for degree credit (from South Puget Sound Community College):
Organic and Biochemistry; Microbiology; Anatomy/Physiology II; Basic First Aid; Basic General Chemistry; Small Group Communications; Nutrition; General Psychology

Relevant courses completed at this institution: Research Methods; Oral Healthcare Research Design Practices I; Field Practice Education Theory/Application; Career Strategies; Field Practice Clinic/Lab Instruction; Field Practice Teach Meth/ Assessment; Oral Healthcare Research Design Practices II; Oral Healthcare Project Implement; Oral Healthcare Project/ Evaluation/Report Writing; Dental Hygiene Capstone

Job Related Training:
Occupational Safety and Health Administration (OSHA) Made Easy: Hazard Communication/Globally Harmonized System and Subparts of the OSHA Regulations (2 Continuing Education Units, or CEUs), 03/2017; Bloodborne Pathogens and Infection Control Made Easy for Dentistry (2 CEUs), 03/2017; Advanced Periodontal Instrumentation, 06/2016; Current Concepts in Oral Medicine, 04/2016; Achieving Your Ideal Position within the Dental Hygiene Profession, 04/2015; Trends in Diagnostic and Treatment of Oral Cancer, 04/2015

Additional Information:

PROFESSIONAL SUMMARY

More than 20 years of experience as a licensed Dental Hygienist with extensive experience in performing expert dental treatment and preventive management. Skilled in performing visual and diagnostic inspections of oral cavities, forming preliminary diagnosis based on tests and imaging results, and collaborating with licensed dentists on patient treatment plans and follow-up care. Licensed to assist with anesthesia during oral surgery procedures, and to treat and inspect patients during follow-up visits. Perform various standard oral hygiene procedures, such as tooth and gum cleanings, to remove surface stains, tartar, and plaque; inspection of the tongue and inner cheeks for suspicious lesions; and application of fluoride treatments and sealants. Provide oral and written patient education guidelines regarding preventive oral care, post-operative care, and adjusting to life with dental prosthetics. Contribute to community activities related to promoting strong oral hygiene practices.

ADDITIONAL EXPERIENCE:

Dental Hygienist, Office of Jack Jackson, Doctor of Dental Surgery (DDS), Creed, WA, 11/2005 to 07/2009
Oral and Maxillofacial/Anesthesia Assistant, Office of Shane Sorenson, DDS, Bunkie, LA, 02/2000 to 10/2005

ACTIVE PROFESSIONAL LICENSES AND CERTIFICATIONS:

Registered Dental Hygienist, State of Washington, valid through 02/17/2018; Licensed Dental Hygienist, State of Minnesota, valid through 02/28/2016; Registered Expanded Functions for Local Anesthesia Administration, State of Washington, State of Minnesota; Registered Restorative Functions Hygienist, State of Washington, State of Minnesota; Certified in the Administration of Local Anesthesia and in Nitrous Oxide Analgesia, State of Washington, State of Minnesota; Cardiopulmonary Resuscitation (CPR) and Automated External Defibrillator (AED) Certified

SUPERVISOR QUOTES AND CUSTOMER COMMENTARY:

"[Maya] has a unique ability to establish rapport with patients quickly. … It's not uncommon for patients to look to her to further explain, validate, or ask for advice on my treatment plans because they trust her professional opinion. … She is skilled in both hygiene and restorative dentistry. The quality of her restorations is comparable to those done by an experienced dentist."
Sheila Drake, Doctor of Dental Surgery (prior supervisor)

COMMUNITY STEWARDSHIP AND VOLUNTEER WORK:

Volunteer, Amigos de los Ninos, Cabo San Lucas, Baja, Mexico (2012, 2016)
Staffed a free, one-week clinic that provided free pediatric dental services to underprivileged and special-needs children.

Student Coordinator, Pierce County Children's Dental Screening and Sealant Day, 04/2015
Developed the program concept and collaborated with fellow students enrolled in Pierce Community College's dental hygienist program and local volunteer dental professionals to provide more than $15K of free dental services and patient education to children of low-income families.

*Orchestrated the scheduling of local dentists willing to donate time to staff the clinic, and negotiated with dental supply companies to donate items to be used both in clinic treatments and to give to patients to take home.

*Served as the Marketing and Promotions Coordinator, tasked with developing and distributing signage promoting the event at local schools, and creating patient documents and oral health educational materials.

ADDITIONAL QUALIFICATIONS:

Ability to communicate effectively, both orally and in writing; anatomic sciences; pathology microbiology-immunology; pharmacology; patient assessment; restorative dentistry; radiology; gerodontics; general dentistry, pediatric dentistry, orthodontic dentistry, endodontic dentistry, oral surgery dentistry, periodontic dentistry, prosthodontic dentistry, pathology dentistry; fluoride treatments; ceramic braces; teeth whitening; composite bonding; soft tissue regeneration; tooth contouring; oral sedation; general anesthesia; local anesthesia; cold sore treatment; neuromuscular dentistry; lumineers; wisdom teeth extractions; sleep apnea therapy; implants; fillings; bruxism appliances; partials; patient education; oral cancer screenings; root canals; dental implants; IV Sedation; digital X-rays; patient appointment scheduling, HIPAA/patient privacy; lab work coordination; pharmaceuticals; treatment room preparation; instrument sterilization; dental supply management; insurance billing; patient literature and resources development; bloodborne and airborne pathogens

Familiar in the use of the following tools: rotating caps; caries detection aids; Neodymium-doped Yttrium Aluminum Garnet (Nd:YAG) dental lasers; calculus explorers; caries explorers; nabers furcation probes; periodontal probes; periapical films; saliva ejectors; suctioning equipment; hand scalers; ultrasonic scalers aspirating syringes; dental needles; panoramic dental X-ray units; intraoral dental cameras; mercury blood pressure units and blood pressure cuffs; microscope slides; nitrous oxide administration equipment; oxygen administration equipment; air-driven dental polishers; air/water syringes; dental polishers; high- and slow-speed dental drills

PRIVATE SECTOR TO GS-9: PROGRAM SPECIALIST

> Client was seeking a GS-9 position as a Program Specialist. Leveraged background as a business owner, retail manager, and operations manager to focus this federal resume for a program specialist/management position.

Mary Porter
22 F Street
Pittsburgh, PA 09627 US
Day Phone: 123-456-7890 - Ext:
Email: myname@hotmail.com

Work Experience:
U.S. Navy
Naval Air Station
Amelia Island, FL   32034 United States

06/2017 - Present
Hours per week: 35
Volunteer

Duties, Accomplishments and Related Skills:
PROGRAM MANAGEMENT: Co-develop suitable strategies and objectives, and advise management and administrative team on the implementation of the same. Prepare and complete action plans, to include developing effective strategies and tactics. Formulate, coordinate, and monitor interconnected assignments and activities. Monitor and provide input to progress of operations. Assess program performance with goal of maximizing return on investment. Resolve problems, identify trends, determine improvements, and implement changes.

ORGANIZATIONAL LEADERSHIP: Lead and facilitate communication and interaction among assigned co-workers. Adhere to master plans and schedules; develop solutions to program problems, and direct work of personnel. Mentor newly assigned volunteers and staff in understanding job description, requirements, policies, and procedures. Act as advisor to program team regarding tasks and operations. Volunteer for additional responsibilities and special undertakings. Update management and staff on status of the same, to include any issues encountered and overall progress.

OPERATIONAL FOCUS: Achieve operational objectives by contributing information and recommendations to strategic plans and reviews. Co-develop new business and product line expansion. Enhance department and organization reputation by accepting ownership for accomplishing new and different requests. Explore opportunities to add value to job accomplishments. Update job knowledge by attending educational opportunities, reading professional publications, maintaining personal networks, and participating in professional organizations.

CUSTOMER SERVICE: Identify and assess customers' needs to achieve satisfaction. Act as liaison by providing product/services information and resolving emerging problems with customer. Build sustainable relationships and trust with customer accounts through open and interactive communication. Empathize with customer and advocate for them, when necessary. Implement production, productivity, quality, and customer-service standards. Ensure prompt delivery of customer service. Respond efficiently to customer inquiries and maintain high customer satisfaction.

ACCOMPLISHMENTS:
*Orchestrated the reorganization of stockroom and loan locker merchandise for more successful inventory and cycle counts.
*Consistently accomplish 100% of projects and tasks assigned daily.
*Successfully increased Fleet and Family Support Center participation by providing product knowledge and outfitting suggestions to patrons.
*Cited by supervisor saying that staff feels that they can rely on organizational skills and attention to detail.
*Rated in top 5% of peers.

Rotary Club, District 8888
123 Main Street
Charleston, SC   55555 United States

05/2013 - 05/2017
Hours per week: 48
Secretary

Duties, Accomplishments and Related Skills:
MANAGEMENT ASSISTANCE: Assisted with preparation and dissemination of materials and agendas for meetings and gave proper notice of the same. Recorded minutes of meetings and accuracy, availability, and approval. Managed organization's records, including founding and governing documents, insurance policies, contracts, committee lists, and other official records to evaluate program productivity. Reviewed and updated documents, as necessary, and ensured safe storage and ready accessibility of the same. Proposed and implemented policies and practices. Supported work of upper management in other areas, when required.

OPERATIONAL FOCUS: Maintained records of organization, as required by law and made available when required by authorized persons. Ensured maintenance and update of official records on members of organization. Ensured availability of records when required for reports, referenda, or votes. Ensured availability of current copy of bylaws at all meetings. Ensured proper notification of meetings, as specified in bylaws. Retained authorization to sign or countersign checks, correspondence, applications, reports, contracts, or other documents on behalf of organization.

ACCOMPLISHMENTS:
*Founding member of this chapter and attended organizational leadership training.
*Developed initiatives of promoting beauty of cultural diversity, raising awareness within local communities on needs of youth at local schools, and community service outreach.
*Mentored local youth on entrepreneurship, leadership, and power of serving community.
*Co-planned organizational fundraisers.
*Coordinated successful event to promote Rotary with City Mayor in attendance.
*Actively sought out for operations, training, and personnel advice throughout organization.

Click Hair Spa
123 Anywhere Street
Houston, TX   55555 United States

06/2011 - 04/2013
Salary: 51,840.00 USD Per Year

Hours per week: 48
Business Owner/Manager/Operator

Duties, Accomplishments and Related Skills:

PROGRAM MANAGEMENT: Ensured smooth operation of salon, security of rooms, reception area, and monitoring of appointments. Worked with stylists in reordering of stock. Exercised control of stock levels, including inventories, purchase orders, and receipt of deliveries. Managed computer system for client records and stock control. Ensured security of all stock, equipment, and monies. Established realistic and commercial targets and monitor progress toward the same. Managed marketing and competition budgets. Enhanced retailing presence in all areas to increase revenue. Ensured effective management of client base.

ORGANIZATIONAL LEADERSHIP: Used initiative when making decisions. Maintained composure and professional deportment when faced with working under pressure. Dealt with problems in calm manner. Maintained motivational speaking skills and set example to staff during team meetings and one-on-one discussions. Exercised interpersonal communication skills in identifying personal issues and difficulties with staff members, which affected work and proposed solutions. Dealt with difficult salon situations, to include client complaints and staff disagreements in a diplomatic manner.

OPERATIONAL FOCUS: Hired and managed staff of stylists and other employees. Engaged in marketing and salon design. Acquired office space, designed, and decorated salon. Developed marketing campaign to advertise services. Ensured cleanliness and sanitation of business area. Verified all employees had current licenses and certifications. Prepared chemicals, products, and equipment for hairdressing treatments and dispensed the quantities needed. Prepared sterilized cabinets and associated materials and equipment for salon sessions.

CUSTOMER SERVICE: Maintained strong client base and ensured customer satisfaction. Greeted customers upon entry to salon, making eye contact and showing genuine interest in their beauty care needs. Engaged clients in friendly conversation. Addressed any disgruntled client with polite and apologetic response while attempting to resolve issue. Handled customer complaints, provided appropriate solutions, and followed up to ensure resolution. Maintained and updated records of customer interactions, processed customer accounts and filed documents. Followed communication procedures, guidelines, and policies.

ACCOMPLISHMENTS:
*Actively sought out for operations, training, and personnel advice throughout organization.
*Cited by client as organized, efficient, and extremely competent, with excellent rapport with people of all ages. Recommended for any position or endeavor; would be valuable asset for any organization.
*Cited by client as "Commendable" in attention to detail and ability to organize training classes. Recommended to teach classes as it relates to hair beauty and health.
*Cited by client as creative, hard-working, with great technical skills, and "will be an asset to any organization."

University of New Orleans
624 Fielding Avenue
New Orleans, LA   77777 United States

11/2009 - 06/2011
Salary: 31,200.00 USD Per Year
Hours per week: 25

Career Planning and Placement Center Coordinator

Duties, Accomplishments and Related Skills:

PROGRAM MANAGEMENT/CAREER SERVICES AND PLACEMENT: Directed and managed university career services as it assisted all student, alumni, faculty, and employer clients in development of career education, career identification, and search, and pursuit of employment opportunities commensurate with formal academic pursuits. Continually expanded client/user base and scope of services to ensure provision of widest array of services possible to broadest mix of academic and corporate clients. Developed efficient strategies and tactics. Achieved operational objectives by contributing recommendations to strategic plans and reviews.

ORGANIZATIONAL LEADERSHIP: Developed new contacts with external organizations to expand employment opportunities for students and alumni. Monitored, analyzed, and evaluated current scope of services offered through career services. Planned, implemented, and directed new programs. Served in leadership role in various professional organizations to include regional affiliates, which provide broad opportunities for job development activities. Provided guidance and leadership to staff, to include training, staff evaluation, professional development, and related personnel matters.

OPERATIONAL FOCUS: Served as advisor and interfaced with representatives of industrial, governmental, and educational employers to ascertain most effective use of career services' efforts. Coordinated and supervised staff professional development activities and training, to include travel for professional development workshops, seminars, and conferences. Managed the operational, budget, and personnel functions of the career services office. Communicated with deans, department chairs, and other faculty to ensure career services department was meeting the needs and desires of the academic colleges and departments.

ACCOMPLISHMENTS:
*Qualified candidates with proper employers, resulting in 80% success rate.
*Actively sought out for operations, training, and personnel advice throughout organization.

Walgreens
12 4th Street
Mesquite, NV   99999 United States

05/2006 - 10/2009
Salary: 27,040.00 USD Per Year
Hours per week: 60
Retail Training Management Intern

Duties, Accomplishments and Related Skills:

MANAGEMENT TRAINING/TECHNICAL ACUMEN: Worked projects and tasks in support role with experienced manager. Managed sales team, conducted personal selling to customers, and explored all facets of business operations. Learned about floor responsibilities to become expert in management field. Recruited and motivated staff. Spent time in each major store department or role with heavy emphasis on learning all facets of store operation. Concentrated on duties, to include, application review and interviewing, new employee training, inventory control, merchandising, employee supervision and evaluation, and various types of recordkeeping.

ORGANIZATIONAL LEADERSHIP: Worked with other managers to plan and direct work of organization and co-developed policies. Worked in different departments to gain perspective, to include marketing, sales, customer services, purchasing, merchandising, and personnel departments. Participated with store management in interviewing, hiring, and training employees. Reported market activity to management by monitoring and analyzing competitive price lists and products. Worked with and through management to develop and implement actions that protected company assets and profitability.

OPERATIONAL FOCUS: Received feedback and critique from Store Manager and executed the same. Examined company reports to analyze sales, gross profit, and inventory activity. Identified trends and recommended proactive or remedial action to manage business situations. Attended lectures, observed guest speakers, and created projects and oral presentations. Managed career services operation to ensure efficient, timely, and effective programs and services to users. Developed short- and long-range operating plans, to include budgets, programs, services, personnel, and technology.

CUSTOMER SERVICE: Greeted customers and provided enjoyable shopping experience for all. Responded to customer requests in a timely manner. Handled and resolved customer complaints. Adhered to execution of established safety, security, quality, and store operations policies, procedures, and practices. Replenished products and supplies to ensure presence of stockage at all times. Checked expiration codes and inspected all items once during shift. Properly rotated product, pulled expired items, documented, and discarded. Communicated with management team regarding customer requests and vendor-related concerns.

ACCOMPLISHMENTS:
*Successfully reorganized photo department and implemented company standards, which resulted in passing a surprise inspection.
*Conducted research projects, on-the-job training, and mystery shopping.
*Completed written projects and research topics on customer service and the effects of different display on increasing sales.

Education:
Texas Southern University Houston, TX United States
Bachelor's Degree 05/2009
GPA: 3.5 of a maximum 4.0
Credits Earned: 120 Semester hours
Major: Business Administration Honors: Cum Laude

Job Related Training:
Ten Steps to Federal Employment, 2018; Career Technical Track, 2016; Leadership Training, 2016; Walgreen's Retail Management Internship Program, 2013; Family Counseling Class, Positive Adult Living, Inc., 2010

Affiliations:
Project Management Institute - Member
Professional Beauty Association - Member
National Society of Collegiate Scholars - Member

Additional Information:
Currently hold an active Secret security clearance

PROFESSIONAL SUMMARY:
Multitalented leader with more than 18 years of progressively broader experience working in program management, operations, training, and personnel leadership and mentoring in supervisory positions of increasing responsibility and in a variety of operational scenarios. Demonstrated ability in program management, operations and training, and Human Resources. Possess vast experience in all aspects of personnel leadership. Stand ready to apply knowledge and previously acquired skills. Managed multiple projects, met tight deadlines, and obtained quality results. Provide exceptional training, mentoring, coaching, and support to clients and colleagues.

SELECTED PROFESSIONAL HIGHLIGHTS:
*Dedicated Program Manager and operations professional who thrives in a fast-paced and demanding work environment and possesses expert knowledge to assist others. Actively sought out for advice as senior member in multiple organizations.
*Highly skilled in managing workflow in multiple scenarios while constantly focusing on improving processes, concepts, and procedures.
*Demonstrated Subject Matter Expert in knowledge of program management, operations, and Human Resource Management.
*Possess a strategic and far-reaching vision by looking at the current scenario, visualizing its direction, and planning accordingly.
*Possess significant mentoring, coaching, advisory, and personnel development experience.
*Continually demonstrate professional deportment and set the example for all colleagues to follow.
*Ensure all organizational personnel have a safe and conducive environment in which to work by identifying potential risks and mitigating them, as needed.

ADDITIONAL RELEVANT CAREER EXPERIENCE:
U.S. Army, Network Switching Systems Operator/Maintainer, 1999-2005

PROFESSIONAL LICENSES AND CERTIFICATIONS:
License, Phoenix School of Massage and Holistic Health; Certification, Detox Therapy Consultant, 2016

AWARDS:
Houston's 40 Under 40 Next Generation of Leaders Award, 2016; Lux 2016 Hotel and Spa Award for Best Natural Hair Salon; Army Good Conduct Medal; National Defense Service Medal (2 awards); Global War on Terrorism Service Medal

PRIVATE SECTOR TO GS-15: LAND/PROPERTY MANAGEMENT

This applicant wanted to leverage his leadership and background in the field of mortgage lending and regulatory compliance to land a GS-15 position in an organization such as Housing and Urban Development (HUD).

Jack Linsey
44 Delmar Blvd.
Harrison, NM 91709 US
Day Phone: 123-456-7890 - Ext:
Email: anyone@hotmail.com

_____

Work Experience:
Stratosphere Mortgage Capital LLC
15315 Fairfield Ranch Road
Chino Hills, CA 91709 United States

11/2015 - Present
Salary: 350,000.00 USD Per Year
Hours per week: 40
Senior Managing Director

Duties, Accomplishments and Related Skills:

PROGRAM MANAGEMENT: Direct dynamic investment banking operations encompassing $4.5B worth of Assets Under Management (AUM) via oversight of 17 personnel, including operations, Human Resources, legal, compliance, accountants, and other specialists. Apply honed technical and managerial expertise to set up effective business plans, which incorporated pro-form financials as well as annual budget allocation. Set up program and project milestones to ensure operational fulfillment, including underwriting of agency and non-agency products; acquisitions of agency and non-agency assets and mortgage-servicing rights; and servicing functions of agency and non-agency assets, such as government loan servicing, payment processing, investor reporting, collection techniques and timelines, bankruptcy and foreclosure timelines, loss-mitigation techniques, claims processes, problem loan reports, and watchlists.

BUDGET MANAGEMENT: Manage, analyze, and allocate $4.5M annual budget. Develop future budget via assessment of previous years' spending plans as well as future organization goals, objectives, and plans. Examine funding and reprogramming actions to determine financial implications as well as to consider and implement alternatives, as necessary.

INTERAGENCY COORDINATION: Collaborate extensively with organizations, such as Federal National Mortgage Association (FNMA), or Fannie Mae, Federal Home Loan Mortgage Corp (FHLMC), or Freddie Mac, and Government National Mortgage Association (GNMA), or Ginnie Mae, in order to facilitate the purchase and sale of whole loans, securities, or mortgage-servicing rights in secondary capital markets. Establish and foster positive professional relationships with agencies such as Department of Housing and Urban Development (HUD), Department of Veterans Affairs (VA), and U.S. Department of Agriculture (USDA) to ensure optimal, regulatory compliant execution of government and conventional mortgage transactions.

POLICIES AND PROCEDURES: Research, develop, draft, and enforce myriad comprehensive policies concerning compliance management system, servicing oversight, and vendor management to strictly adhere to governing regulations, such as the Dodd Frank Act and by agencies such as Consumer Financial Protection Bureau, FNMA, FHLMC, and GNMA.

Evaluate impact of changes to laws, regulations, policies, and procedures; adjusted local requirements accordingly.

ACCOMPLISHMENTS:
*Provided superior management to $4.5B of Assets Under Management (AUM).
Supervisor: Nick Franklin (12-555-234)
Okay to contact this Supervisor: Yes

Lending Services, Inc.
100 Drone Drive
Terrytown, LA   55778 United States

12/2013 - 12/2015
Salary: 340,000.00 USD Per Year
Hours per week: 40
President/Chief Executive Officer

Duties, Accomplishments and Related Skills:
PROGRAM MANAGEMENT: Directed, led, and supervised Operations, Sales, Accounting, Compliance, Information Technology, Human Resources, and Loan Servicing to optimize lending operations in highly competitive market. Continually monitored and evaluated plans, products, employees, and operations to meet company standards and production requirements. Directed and organized employees; created employee work schedules; defined priorities and set deadlines; set and adjusted short-term priorities; identified potential problems and determined solutions. Conducted reviews, including qualitative and quantitative analysis of technical problems, policies, and cost/time estimates of man-hours. Managed planning, allocation, auditing, and direction of $80M annual operating budget to effectively support robust lending operations serving both private citizens and businesses.

POLICIES AND PROCEDURES: Oversaw all compliance policies and procedures, including those concerning local application of: Fair Lending, Real Estate Settlement Procedures Act (RESPA), Truth in Lending Act (TILA), Anti-Money Laundering (AML), Home Mortgage Disclosure Act (HMDA), vendor management, Mortgage Local Originator (MLO) compensation, Licensing, Quality Control, Marketing, Marketing Services Agreement (MSA), Internal Audits, State and Agency Audits, Nationwide Multistate Licensing System and Registry (NMLS) call reports, and Loan Servicing.

REVIEW AND ANALYSIS: Analyzed problems to develop decision rules for a program or organization. Evaluated performance goals and measures of policy initiatives affecting the mission. Identified and analyzed problems distinguishing between relevant and irrelevant information to make rational decisions. Used qualitative data and analytical tools in problem solving. Developed procedures and plans for meeting the organization's goals and objectives.

ORAL AND WRITTEN COMMUNICATION: Prepared and presented analytical information to senior management officials within and outside the organization in order to explain or justify decision, conclusions, findings, and recommendations. Developed comprehensive material for reports, briefings, or meetings of senior management officials on issues such as production, regulatory compliance, staffing, training, certifications, and other relevant factors. Elicited and documented both functional and technical requirements in a thorough manner, producing comprehensive work products that demonstrated attention to detail. Justified, persuaded, negotiated, and resolved matters involving significant or controversial policy or program issues via effective, harmonious communications.

ACCOMPLISHMENTS:

*Strategically planned and executed acquisition of lending company, resulting in 10 additional retail branches of 150 employees and driving $1.5B in production volume annually.

*Led senior management team through innovative strategy to expand company from regional producer to national retail and wholesale producer; successfully developed and implemented strategic plan to increase production from $400M annually at regional level to $6B at national level over course of four years.

*Piloted relocation of multiple components of fulfillment operations, resulting in significantly enhanced efficiency and monthly savings of $200K.

Optimal Financial
90 Bark Gulch
East Atlantic Beach, MT   11561 United States

03/2011 - 11/2013
Salary: 180,000.00 USD Per Year
Hours per week: 40
Chief Compliance Officer

Duties, Accomplishments and Related Skills:

PROGRAM ANALYSIS: Analyzed efficiency of financial and administrative operations, organizational management, and specific issues, using analytical methods and techniques for problem resolution in order to effectively manage programs, policies, and operations concerning billions of dollars of lending programs. Compiled, organized, and analyzed data garnered via comprehensive in-house audits to determine company's adherence to governing regulations, such as those of HUD, California Department of Business Oversight. Analyzed the effectiveness of line program operations in meeting established goals and objectives, and in complying with all applicable regulations. Assessed program development and execution to improve organizational effectiveness and efficiency.

QUALITY ASSURANCE: Developed, maintained, and enforced high quality assurance (QA) standards and goals. Inspected work and procedures to ensure quality. Evaluated lending programs versus governing regulations to ensure strict compliance. Collected and analyzed data from a variety of sources to ensure all operations were within QA standards.

AUDITING: Independently conducted program audits. Tested and examined records and accounting systems to assess compliance with accounting principles, contract provisions, and regulations.

REPORTS & DOCUMENTATION: Scheduled, wrote, and properly audited reports. Conducted briefings and presentations to executive management and relevant stakeholders. Wrote objective and responsive reports of investigations and in response to requests for information. Wrote objective and responsive reports of audit findings, conclusions, and recommendations for delivery to the audit requestor. Prepared audit working papers and substantiating documents in accordance with agency requirements. Drafted reports of audit findings, conclusions, and recommendations covering audit assignments for review. Ensured reports were based on facts and supported by substantiating documents and workpapers.

ACCOMPLISHMENTS:

*Oversaw rigorous audit preparation ahead of comprehensive program audits on biennial basis; consistently achieved successful outcomes as a result of superior program management and strict compliance with all governing regulations.

*Served key role in company's national expansion by personally obtaining 13 state Nationwide Multistate Licensing System and Registry licenses, thereby qualifying as Control Officer/Qualifying Individual within senior Management position.

*Researched, developed, and implemented local regulations and processes to ensure organizational compliance to relevant regulations, including those of newly formed Consumer Financial Protection Bureau.

Home Mortgage, Inc.
22 Schweda Drive
Santa Clara, UT   84765 United States

06/2008 - 02/2011
Salary: 200,000.00 USD Per Year
Hours per week: 40
President and CEO

Duties, Accomplishments and Related Skills:
LEADERSHIP AND SUPERVISION: Directed 25 multidisciplinary personnel in performance of establishment and operation of dynamic mortgage services company servicing 2K+ customers and garnering $400M in production annually. Developed, conducted, and reviewed training programs and records to ensure personnel were fully up-to-date on all aspects of financial operations. Conducted counseling, feedback, performance evaluation, and disciplinary actions.

ORAL AND WRITTEN COMMUNICATION: Communicated effectively, both orally and in writing, to inform current and potential clients on mortgage policies and procedures ranging from basic to complex. Utilized clear, concise terms to ensure clients fully understood rules, regulations, procedures, risks, and objectives. Addressed questions and concerns clearly to enable clients to make informed decisions on myriad mortgages. Liaised with federal and non-federal agencies to originate or facilitate specific transactions.

MARKETING: Initiated and developed detailed marketing strategies, publicity plans, programs, and public relations, using marketing research survey methods and data analysis to determine customers' needs. Built relationships and increased business contracts using sales, organizational, motivational, and negotiation skills to promote and market services. Maintained current working knowledge of mortgage and financial industry standards to ensure comparability of marketing/advertising efforts. Identified market requirements to develop appropriate implementation procedures and program guidance for organizational activities.

PROGRAM PLANNING: Oversaw the planning and allocation of $3M annual budget. Conducted extensive research to gather information from multiple sources concerning clients' financial portfolios, mortgage objectives, and resources. Organized and prioritized data and developed optimal lending plan, which would align with all factors, such as current and projected financial resources, limiting factors, goals, and other issues. Organized and planned client presentations to relay information and recommendations to them in clear, concise terms.

INTERPERSONAL SKILLS: Initiated, developed, and fostered strong, trusting working relationships with clients and subordinates to maximize effectiveness of operations. Employed active listening to hear their concerns, past experiences, and overall goals to determine optimal course of lending programs to meet their needs.

EVALUATING INFORMATION AND DECISION MAKING: Collected vast amount of financial data and information on clients' personal financial objectives. Evaluated all factors to include current economic environment and other stated factors in order to ascertain optimal mortgage planning. Heard and responded to clients' requests and determined the feasibility thereof. Used strong interpersonal skills to relay details of why particular strategies would be good decisions and why others would not, ensuring clients' full understanding of reasoning and methodology.

ACCOMPLISHMENTS:
*Established highly successful business, which grew from achieving $500K net worth in less than two years to $400M annually.

Education:
University of Montana Tyler, TX United States
Bachelor's Degree 01/2015
Major: Organizational Management Honors: Cum Laude

Additional Information:
SECURITY CLEARANCE: Secret

PROFESSIONAL SUMMARY:
More than 25 years' experience supporting major lending operations worth billions of dollars agencies as within executive leadership capacity. Recognized and proven capabilities in research and analysis, along with superior project management and interpersonal skills, have enabled vast success in improving multimillion-dollar programs while strictly adhering to governing regulations. Exceptional financial capability, organizational skills, and communication ability led to designation as Subject Matter Expert in all aspects of financial management with the synergistic skills in relaying sound financial advisory services to personnel of all backgrounds and specialties. Expertly manage, review, troubleshoot, and refine multimillion-dollar budgets to enable optimal use of funds. Provide strict monitoring of spending programs to ensure there's no misappropriation of funds and to verify compliance with all federal and state financial rules and regulations.

PROFESSIONAL LICENSES AND CERTIFICATIONS:
*Oregon Principal Lending Manager
*Texas Qualified Individual License
*Mortgage Loan Originator License, CA, FL, NJ, NV, NY, PA, UT

MILITARY EXPERIENCE:
U.S. Navy, 1991-1995, E-5, Petty Officer Second Class, Honorable Discharge

SPECIFIC QUALIFICATIONS:
*Oversee the administration, management, direction, and control of the Loan Guaranty program in the geographic area serviced by the Housing and Urban Development (HUD) and Department of Veterans Affairs (VA)
*Evaluate the impact of changes to laws, regulations, policies, and procedures
*Relay complex information to a variety of audiences
*Ensure staff is fully conversant with applicable laws and customs unique to one or more of the multiple states under their geographic jurisdiction
*Ensure applicable training plans and schedules are developed and made available to all staff
*Define business goals, develop work plans, and set short- and long-term priorities to be accomplished by subordinates
*Direct, coordinate, and oversee work plans through subordinate managers and supervisors. Assign work based on priorities, selective consideration of the difficulty and requirements of assignments, and the capabilities of employees
*Evaluate program implementation and effectiveness
*Provide guidance, advice, counsel, or instruction to subordinates in resolving administrative and on technical problems
*Manage relationships with functional executives of organization's operating divisions within the area serviced, officials of other agencies, and in advising management officials of higher rank
*Develop performance standards and evaluate work performance of subordinate supervisors and managers

---

MILITARY TO GS-5: HUMAN RESOURCES

This applicant served more than eight years in the Army and was seeking a position as Human Resources Assistant, GS-0203-5/7. He focused on demonstrating relevant skills in human resource management, administrative support, and records and report management.

Hayden Milner
222 Deuce Drive
Evanston, WY 11587 US
Day Phone: 123-456-7890 - Ext:
Email: anyone@gmail.com

Work Experience:
4th Infantry Division, United States Army
234 Main Street
Louisville, TN   37777 United States

02/2017 - Present
Salary: 30,427.00 USD Per Year
Hours per week: 40
Human Resources Specialist

Duties, Accomplishments and Related Skills:
HUMAN RESOURCES OPERATIONS: Participate in occupational classification and management of Human Resources (HR), maintaining personnel records and processing personnel actions for service members and their families. Execute personnel service center-level procedures and actions to process classification and reclassification actions and prepare orders and requests for orders. Process leave requests, controlling, processing, and accounting for Request and Authority for Leave forms for submission to Finance Department. Evaluate personnel qualifications for special assignments and prepare and process requests for transfer or reassignment.

PERSONNEL TRAINING AND SUPPORT: Provide support for the trainee management area, including processing and tracking the Personnel Status Report. Process applications for Officer Candidate School, Warrant Officer School, flight training, and other specialized training. Review Personnel Action forms for Army Basic Combat Training graduations and track each graduate in the correct unit in Electronic Military Personnel Office database. Download and distribute Advanced Individual Training orders. Initiate, monitor, and process personnel evaluations and prepare recommendations for awards and decorations. Initiate applications for passports and visas and prepare deployment forms. Process soldiers for reenlistment, separation, and retirement.

RECORDS AND REPORTS: Develop and distribute personnel records, applying knowledge of provisions and limitations of Freedom of Information and Privacy Acts. Prepare reports on staffing levels and the status of available personnel and maintain files on Automatic Data Processing systems. Generate and maintain Officer and enlisted personnel records. Update the total number of personnel weekly and the Post Strength and Personnel Accountability records monthly, ensuring accuracy and timely submission of information. Prepare and review personnel casualty documents and prepare letters of sympathy for next of kin. Produce correspondence and forms in draft and final copy. Post changes to Army regulations and other publications.

KEY ACCOMPLISHMENTS:

*Demonstrated exceptional attention to detail, instrumental in the processing of 1.6K leave requests with 100% account-ability during the 2017 holiday block leave.

*In addition, ensured all Request and Authority for Leave forms were controlled, processed, accounted for, and submitted to Finance Department in a timely manner.

*Hand-selected as Finance Clerk, processing 200 finance transactions for personnel pay.

*Played a key role in 28 Army Basic Combat Training graduations, tracking and reviewing Personnel Action forms; ensured each graduate was placed in the correct unit in the database.

*Processed personnel documents for approximately 5K soldiers in preparation for transfer to respective assigned command.

United States Army
U.S. Personnel Command
Fort Polk, LA   57575 United States

07/2009 - 01/2017
Salary: 30,427.20 USD Per Year
Hours per week: 40
Team Leader

Duties, Accomplishments and Related Skills:

MILITARY OPERATIONS: Participated in training exercises and security operations and provided support to associate personnel to ensure the highest level of security and readiness. Strictly followed orders, security directives, and safety regulations and demonstrated spirit of teamwork and cooperation.

PERSONNEL SUPPORT OPERATIONS: Served as an HR Specialist in the staffing section, playing a vital role within a short-notice section. Received, issued, and processed hazardous duty orders, ensuring appropriate pay in a timely manner. Served as the Finance Clerk and Customer Service Clerk during tenure with the staffing section, making daily trips to the finance processing center to ensure all actions were processed on time.

LEADERSHIP AND SUPPORT: Worked closely with each Commander to ensure compliance with unit command finance report requirements. Served as the Customer Service Clerk, receiving all actions from the paratroopers in the squadron as well as providing guidance and advice to leadership and associates. Deployed to Afghanistan from 11/2009 to 12/2010, completing day-and-night combat patrols and key leader engagements. Mentored Afghan National Army (ANA) soldiers in proper firing techniques, and the search of local national individuals, vehicles, and enemy combatants.

KEY ACCOMPLISHMENTS:

*Received, issued, and processed more than 300 hazardous duty orders, enabling the paratroopers to receive appropriate pay.

Supervisor: Douglass Hall (011-49-9641-83-9533)
Okay to contact this Supervisor: Yes

Education:
Delgado College Marrero, LA United States
Bachelor's Degree 12/2014
Major: Business Administration

Job Related Training:

Network Security Course, 09/2017
Personal Computer Components Course, 09/2017
Laptop Components, Peripherals, and Networks Course, 09/2015
Operating Systems Course, 09/2015
Security, Safety, and Communication Course, 09/2015
Working with Laptops and Portable Devices Course, 09/2015
Understanding and Maintaining Networks Course, 09/2015
Human Resources Specialist Course, 10/2014
Information Security and Risk Management Course, 09/2014
Operations Security Course, 09/2014
Legal, Regulations, Compliance, and Investigation Course, 09/2014
Security Management and Operations Security Procedures Course, 09/2014

Additional Information:
SECURITY CLEARANCE: Secret

PROFESSIONAL SUMMARY: Highly motivated, accomplished, and results-driven professional with leadership experience in personnel and administrative support and professional development. Hands-on experience analyzing, planning, and coordinating administrative support for Human Resources (HR) operations. Work efficiently, with no direct supervision, multitasking and responding rapidly to changing circumstances. Demonstrated skills in evaluating problems, making astute decisions, and refocusing on new priorities to ensure highest level of operational effectiveness and efficiency.

HUMAN RESOURCES AND ADMINISTRATIVE EXPERTISE: Provide guidance related to workforce planning and efficiency, planning workloads and adjusting priorities and assignments to meet constantly changing organizational needs. Demonstrate knowledge of administrative and management principles involved in personnel planning, resource allocation, HR actions, and personnel development. Prepare and deliver training, ensuring training program provides the competencies necessary to deliver exceptional service to customers. Apply knowledge of administrative and clerical procedures and systems, such as word processing, files and records management, forms design, and office procedures and terminology. Skill in researching, preparing, and presenting reports, briefings, information papers, and personnel summaries.

OFFICE OPERATIONS AND EQUIPMENT: Extensive knowledge of the capabilities and functions of a variety of office equipment and software, including word processors, spreadsheets, databases, graphics, and telecommunications applicable to office and administrative duties. Apply knowledge of databases and related programs used to store and compile vast amounts of data.

COMMUNICATION: Skillfully and effectively relay information, both verbally and in writing, arranging thoughts and judgments to clearly project ideas and achieve maximum results. Develop presentation to suit the audience, ensuring participation and comprehension. Highly responsive to requests for help and information; effectively listen to concerns of customers and resolve complaints and concerns promptly.

COMPUTER SKILLS: Microsoft (MS) Windows Operating Systems; MS Software (Word, Excel, Outlook, and Internet Explorer); Electronic Military Personnel Office database

AWARDS: Army Achievement Medal (3); Army Commendation Medal (2)

MILITARY TO GS-7: VETERANS SERVICE REPRESENTATIVE

> This Navy service member was pending retirement and seeking to gain a position as a Veterans Service Representative (VSR) at the GS-7 level. His program management, communication, and customer-service skills were emphasized throughout the resume.

Jennifer Shanahan
9009 Redwood Road
Salt Lake City, UT 84115 US
Day Phone: 123-456-7890 - Ext:
Email: anyone@gmail.com

Work Experience:
Center for Industrial Studies, U.S. Navy
16 Opelousas Ave.
Longdale, OK   73755 United States

03/2016 - Present
Salary: 50,868.00 USD Per Year
Hours per week: 40
Individual Material Readiness Manager

Duties, Accomplishments and Related Skills:
Oversee inventory control and coordinate movement of U.S. Navy assets valued at more than $37.5M.

PROGRAM MANAGEMENT: Serve as the Program Manager and primary Point of Contact for the Individual Material Readiness List (IMRL) and Command Managed Equal Opportunity (CMEO) programs. Interview and evaluate candidates for the CMEO Program. Provide consultative advice and assistance to senior leadership to provide full and comprehensive explanations of program decisions or recommendations. Collect program feedback on issues and procedural matters through annual surveys; analyze responses and establish focus groups to evaluate issues and make recommendations for improvement. Serve as Facilities Manager and support renovation contracts for five facilities valued at more than $1M.

INVENTORY CONTROL: Supervise inventory management and control of more than 2.1K products. Maintain 100% accountability for inventory of nine departments in three locations. Coordinate and oversee annual physical inventory. Maintain custody records for all inventory and submit reports for all lost, stolen, or missing inventory items. Identify excess inventory and solicit disbursement or disposal instructions from senior leadership. Coordinate submission of inventory revision requests to support organizational requirements.

LEADERSHIP & TRAINING: Explain benefit programs and entitlement criteria to personnel. Refer personnel to other federal, state, and local agencies for support services. Work with subordinate personnel to establish and achieve daily, monthly, weekly, and annual career advancement priorities. Provide training to new personnel.

COMMUNICATION & CUSTOMER SERVICE: Conduct interviews in person and by telephone. Prepare and deliver oral and written career counseling to subordinate personnel. Lead and participate in daily, weekly, and quarterly meetings.

Release requested information with strict adherence to regulations established by the Privacy Act, Freedom of Information Act (FOIA), and Health Insurance Portability and Accountability Act (HIPAA).
ACCOMPLISHMENTS:
*Overhauled inventory control procedures for more than 2.1K items, resulting in 100% accountability, with zero lost, stolen, or missing items.

*Received and inventoried 350 high-value items for inaugural $256.5M Boeing maritime patrol aircraft.

*Led CMEO Program to achieve highest designation of being fully compliant, with no deficiencies noted, during Inspector General evaluation.

U.S. Navy
USS Commissioned Ship
Lanark Village, FL 32323 United States

09/2013 - 02/2016
Salary: 48,993.00 USD Bi-weekly
Hours per week: 60
Ground Support Equipment Manager

Duties, Accomplishments and Related Skills:
Coordinated maintenance of ground support equipment for U.S. Navy organization, including maintenance of more than 1.4K equipment items during a seven-month deployment in the Western Pacific Ocean.

PROGRAM MANAGEMENT: Supervised maintenance program and procedures for more than 200 types of aircraft engines and modules and 1.1K ground support and aircraft weapons equipment. Effectively managed maintenance priorities by developing daily schedules based on constantly changing requirements and factors. Supervised more than 55 maintenance personnel in the completion of more than 12.8K staffing hours. Coordinated nearly 1.7K maintenance actions in support of organizational requirements. Applied process improvement methodologies, including Lean Six Sigma, to increase program efficiency. Ensured maintenance documentation procedures were completed consistently and accurately by all team members. Ensured program compliance with governing regulations and organizational policy.

LEADERSHIP & TRAINING: Determined workload requirements and made personnel assignments to meet program and project requirements. Coordinated and monitored all maintenance activities for program. Explained benefit programs and entitlement criteria to personnel. Updated daily production reports. Developed daily, monthly, weekly, and annual professional growth priorities for subordinate personnel. Mentored more than 55 subordinate personnel and contributed to the professional advancement of 15 personnel.

COMMUNICATION & CUSTOMER SERVICE: Mentored subordinate personnel with oral and written career counseling. Released requested information with strict adherence to regulations established by the Privacy Act and FOIA. Communicated regularly with Program Director to establish work plans to accomplish maintenance and logistic readiness tasks. Served as liaison between Maintenance Program and Production Division to coordinate scheduled and unscheduled maintenance on a wide range of aircraft components and weapons and ground support equipment. Addressed and resolved technical and mechanical issues.

ACCOMPLISHMENTS:
*Expertly led team of 27 personnel to perform maintenance on more than 500 items of support equipment during three-month scheduled maintenance period.
*Oversaw the assembly, repair, and load test certification of aircraft crash handling and salvage crane capable of lifting more than 75K pounds; ensured 100% support of organizational requirements.
*Directed team of technical personnel in performing maintenance on 25% of support equipment inventory; maintained an impeccable safety record and completed work ahead of schedule.
*Provided training to more than 100 personnel, contributing to overall success of organization meeting personnel certification requirements.

U.S. Navy
USS Commissioned Ship
Norfolk, VA   22222 United States

01/2009 - 08/2013
Salary: 48,993.00 USD Bi-weekly
Hours per week: 60
Industrial Hygiene Technician/Safety Department Supervisor

Duties, Accomplishments and Related Skills:
Oversaw safety and industrial hygiene programs for more than 5K U.S. Navy personnel.

PROGRAM MANAGEMENT: Coordinated maintenance activities to ensure operational readiness for organizational missions and requirements. Ensured safety of more than 5K personnel by evaluating 62 work centers to prevent injuries caused by physical and chemical agents. Oversaw administration of safety program for more than 5K personnel. Supervised 165 safety managers in 21 Occupational Safety and Health programs. Directed maintenance and production activities in three work centers. Conducted 48 occupational health surveys. Performed more than 60 safety and industrial hygiene evaluations for newly established work centers.

LEADERSHIP & TRAINING: Explained benefit programs and entitlement criteria to personnel. Collaborated with subordinate personnel to establish daily, monthly, weekly, and annual priorities for professional development. Monitored safety training for more than 5K personnel. Implemented training course for safety managers, resulting in the qualification of 74 new managers.

COMMUNICATION & CUSTOMER SERVICE: Provided oral and written career counseling to subordinate personnel. Released requested information with strict adherence to regulations established by the Privacy Act and FOIA.

ACCOMPLISHMENTS:
*Oversaw the successful and safe collection of more than 60 asbestos and lead samples to support habitability projects.
*Skillfully trained and qualified more than 110 shipboard safety managers, resulting in a 98% qualification rate for the entire organization.
*Led four safety committee meetings with 165 safety management personnel, resulting in a 34% decrease in accidents and mishaps.
*Directly contributed to more than 2K accident-free aircraft moves, safe execution of 1.2K aircraft elevator operations, and secure movement of more than 1K tons of aviation weaponry in a six-month period.

Education:
University of Dakota Newton Falls, OH United States
Bachelor's Degree 12/2017
Major: Psychology Minor: Women's Studies

Job Related Training:
Command Management Equal Opportunity Program Training, U.S. Navy, 2016
Casualty Assistance Calls Officer Training, U.S. Navy, 2016
Leadership Course, U.S. Navy, 2013
Respiratory Protection Program Management Training, U.S. Navy, 2012
Exposure Monitor Course, U.S. Navy, 2012
Support Equipment Asset Manager Training, U.S. Navy, 2012
Aircraft Crash and Salvage Crane Training, U.S. Navy, 2011
Recruit Division Commander, U.S. Navy, 2008
Journeyman Instructor Training, U.S. Navy, 2008

Additional Information:
PROFESSIONAL SUMMARY:

Accomplished Program Manager and U.S. Navy veteran with more than 22 years of experience providing exceptional support to U.S. military logistics programs. Results-driven Program Manager and Safety Specialist responsible for more than 2K accident-free aircraft moves, safe execution of 1.2K aircraft elevator operations, secure movement of more than 1K tons of aviation weaponry, and a 34% reduction in accidents and injuries. U.S. Navy veteran who has expertly mentored and trained thousands of personnel. Versatile Logistics Specialist who has maintained meticulous inventory control for assets valued at more than $30.5M. Now poised to leverage proven program managements skills, vast military leadership experience, and administrative expertise to help the U.S. Department of Veterans Affairs meet and exceed its organizational and operational goals.

PROFESSIONAL HIGHLIGHTS:

*Overhauled inventory control procedures for more than 2.1K items, resulting in 100% accountability, with zero lost, stolen, or missing items.
*Received and inventoried 350 high-value items for inaugural $256.5M Boeing P-8 Poseidon maritime patrol aircraft.
*Led Command Managed Equal Opportunity Program to achieve highest designation of being fully compliant, with no deficiencies noted, during Inspector General evaluation.
*Expertly led team of 27 personnel to perform maintenance on more than 500 items of support equipment during three-month scheduled maintenance period in Atsugi, Japan.
*Oversaw the assembly, repair, and load test certification of aircraft crash handling and salvage crane capable of lifting more than 75K pounds; ensured 100% support of organizational requirements.
*Directed team of technical personnel in performing maintenance on 25% of support equipment inventory; maintained an impeccable safety record and completed work ahead of schedule.
*Collaborated with 60-person Damage Control Training Team to provide training to more than 100 personnel, contributing to overall success of organization meeting personnel certification requirements.

SUPERVISOR QUOTES AND CUSTOMER COMMENTARY:

"Displaying exceptional leadership, she spearheaded weekly and quarterly departmental safety meetings and trained 150 departmental and divisional safety petty officers, expediting full qualifications for all safety petty officers onboard U.S.S. George Washington, improving from 28% to 98% in preparation for the 2012 board of inspection and survey. Additionally,

as Assistant Respiratory Protection Program Manager, he qualified 550 sailors in the proper use of respiratory equipment, minimizing adverse health effects related to chemical and particulate hazards."
- Cited from official 2017 U.S. Navy Performance Appraisal

AWARDS:
Navy/Marine Corps Commendation Medal
Navy/Marine Corps Achievement Medal (4)
Humanitarian Service Medal (2)
Good Conduct Medal (7)
Navy/Marine Corps Overseas Service Ribbon (5)
Sea Service Deployment Ribbon (3)

MILITARY EXPERIENCE:
U.S. Navy, 07/1999 to Present, Chief Petty Officer, E7

SPECIFIC QUALIFICATIONS:
Effective team leader; Inventory control expertise; Meticulous attention to detail; Familiar with military regulations and policy; Possess more than 17 years of military service; Experience with Naval Tactical Command Support System (NTCSS) logistics software suite, Naval Aviation Logistics Command Management Information System (NALCOMIS), and NTCSS NALCOMIS Optimized Intermediate Maintenance Activity (IMA); Effectively manage priorities; Experience with Microsoft Office software, including Word, Excel, PowerPoint, Access, and Outlook; Communicate effectively, both orally and in writing

MILITARY TO GS-12: HR SPECIALIST/PROGRAM ANALYST

> With a background in HR, this service member wanted to attain a GS-12 position as an HR Specialist or Management/Program Analyst. The resume focuses on his relevant personnel administration and management experience.

Milt Dixon
95 Old Roundhouse Drive
Joshua, OR 76542 US
Day Phone: 123-456-7890 - Ext:
Email: anyone@gmail.com

_____

Work Experience:
U.S. Army
Headquarters
Washington DC, DC 20227 United States

05/2016 - Present
Salary: 89,448.00 USD Per Year
Hours per week: 50
Human Resources Staff Mentor

Duties, Accomplishments and Related Skills:
Advised organizational director and staff sections on all matters relating to Human Resources (HR) issues and hiring strategies (accessions) to include personnel management and administration, manpower allocation, and welfare of assigned service members.

HUMAN RESOURCE MANAGEMENT: Served as the Point of Contact in voting assistance (assisting personnel on obtaining an absentee voting ballot from their voting precinct in the U.S.) and promoting the Combined Federal Campaign (CFC) program—a voluntary, annual charitable giving program for all service members. Recommended improvements to already-established HR processes to improve efficiency and effectiveness. Managed and executed all aspects of administrative support in a wartime environment, to include personnel actions, awards, discipline, personnel management and accountability, Rest and Recuperation leave, and evaluations.

OPERATIONAL FOCUS/PROGRAM ANALYSIS: Planned, developed, and coordinated planning management through briefings, presentations, and conferences for executive management. Identified and used best practices to efficiently and effectively identify and manage risks and issues. Analyzed and transitioned the HR section from one organizational entity to another newly configured coalition-planning element in support of Operation Enduring Freedom. Analyzed program policies and information on Voting Awareness Program and the CFC to become the organization's Subject Matter Expert (SME) in these areas. Disseminated information on each to all organizational members, preparing to research and answer all questions about the same.

ACCOMPLISHMENTS:
*Planned and executed the celebration of more than 20 inbound and outbound coalition unit members to include organizing biographies, awards, combat patches, and gifts.
*Personally improved the Command's personnel accountability capability.

*Interfaced with external organizations, which had a lasting effect on organizational ability to identify and provide preparatory deployment training.
*Actively sought out for personnel advice throughout organization.
*Cited by superior as a mission-focused Officer and dedicated to caring about his personnel.

U.S. Army
Headquarters
Washington, DC   20227 United States

12/2014 - 04/2016
Salary: 89,448.00 USD Per Year
Hours per week: 50
Personnel Branch Chief

Duties, Accomplishments and Related Skills:
HUMAN RESOURCE MANAGEMENT: Supervised and directed four personnel. Developed planning strategies and managed the operations of HR reception, replacement, return to duty, redeployment, casualty, and postal duties in conjunction with providing support to the organization's Area of Responsibility. Identified issues in established HR processes, provided guidance and recommendations on improvements, and reengineered processes. Provided technical guidance to six HR Support Operations Centers (SOCs) in personnel accountability, casualty, and postal duties as well as to the parent organization overall.

OPERATIONAL FOCUS/PROGRAM ANALYSIS: Identified and used best practices to identify and manage risks and issues efficiently and effectively. Maintained focus, identified critical tasks, and set priorities accordingly. Shared best practices, training objectives, and cost-saving measures within all SOCs across Sustainment (logistical) Community. Drafted communications pieces, including articles, presentations, and email messages. Wrote final documents covering information, such as policies, training manuals, and management reports to executive-level officials.

ACCOMPLISHMENTS:
*Selected to be the organization's Operations Planner in Afghanistan for six months.
*Assisted external units while simultaneously furthering the development of the annual plan.
*Saved U.S. government several thousands of dollars in training costs, 2nd Quarter of Fiscal Year (FY) 2013.

U.S. Army
Office of Security Cooperation
Kabul, Afghanistan

07/2012 - 11/2014
Salary: 87,720.00 USD Bi-weekly
Hours per week: 50
Administrative Advisor

Duties, Accomplishments and Related Skills:
HUMAN RESOURCE MANAGEMENT: Advised multiple coalition military organizations on personnel and administrative matters. Developed systems providing advice to client Iraqi Army counterparts, to include administrative tracking, processing, and management of more than 7K Iraqi soldiers. Advised client administrative personnel on best practices for

achieving resolution on the exact number of soldiers within organization, to include subordinate organizations. Recommended improvements to already-established HR processes to improve efficiency and effectiveness. Advised on projecting future personnel needs and development of career management for all ranks within the organizations.

OPERATIONAL FOCUS/PROGRAM ANALYSIS: Planned, developed, and coordinated planning management through briefings, presentations, and conferences for executive management. Participated in special studies. Assisted project teams supporting the identification and resolution of HR issues within the client arena. Organized and coordinated thorough, systematic, and professional efforts to meet complex planning needs. Provided clear and accurate oral presentations and updates to own chain of command. Wrote final documents covering complex information, such as policies, training manuals, observations, and final evaluation on client abilities to senior-level officials.

ACCOMPLISHMENTS:
*Improved client personnel systems and procedures for more than 7K personnel by establishing a previously nonexistent personnel roster, replete with all relevant information covering all client organizations assigned to multiple locations throughout Iraq.
*Tracked and audited the Iraqi procedures and systems for Mortuary Affairs (MA), in-/out-processing, awards and promotions, and strength accounting procedures.
*Worked at one level above present rank, consistently demonstrating initiative and commitment to the mission. Cited by one superior that level of maturity emulated that of seasoned higher-ranking Officer.
*Ranked by superior in the top 25% of administrative officers with whom he had served throughout his career.

U.S. Army
Headquarters
Washington , DC   20227 United States

01/2009 - 06/2012
Salary: 87,720.00 USD Bi-weekly
Hours per week: 60
HR Team Leader

Duties, Accomplishments and Related Skills:
HUMAN RESOURCE MANAGEMENT: Directed and supervised 12 HR professionals. SME in the personnel accountability, casualty, and postal missions, as required. Shared best logistical practices across the Sustainment Community that collectively prepared and trained logistical organization for deployment as well as improving their installation (base) sustainment readiness. Recommended improvements to already-established HR processes to improve efficiency and effectiveness. Assisted multiple subordinate units in identifying and resolving complex HR issues.

OPERATIONAL FOCUS/PROGRAM ANALYSIS: Provided expert advice to executive managers, and developed and evaluated policies and programs in assigned program areas. Planned, developed, and coordinated planning management through briefings, presentations, and conferences for executive management. Researched, developed, and implemented HR program evaluation plans, procedures, and best practices. Planned and participated in practices supporting HR programs while advising senior-level management. Developed HR program improvements. Provided alternative solutions and recommended actions to achieve program objectives.

ACCOMPLISHMENTS:
*Gathered and shared best practices and cost savings and saved the Army tens of millions of dollars in FYs 2011 and 2012.

*Provided relevant information to organizations in need to save money and avoid costs by using military personnel instead of civilian contractors for contracted sustainment operations.

Education:
Shaw University Tyler, TX United States
Master's Degree 08/2017
GPA: 2.67 of a maximum 4.0
Credits Earned: 36 Semester hours
Major: Religious Education

Sunrise College Macon, GA United States
Bachelor's Degree 12/2002
GPA: 3.19 of a maximum 4.0
Credits Earned: 60 Semester hours
Major: Religious Education Minor: History

Job Related Training:
Open Water Diver, Professional Association of Diving Instructors (PADI) Certification, 2016

Additional Information:
Currently hold an active Secret security clearance

PROFESSIONAL SUMMARY:
Multitalented leader with more than 19 years of progressively broader experience working in Human Resources (HR) Management, program analysis, and personnel leadership in supervisory positions of increasing responsibility and in a variety of operational scenarios. Possess vast experience and demonstrated ability in all HR management policies and procedures. Possess extraordinarily strong organizational skills. Able to work effectively in a fast paced, high-energy environment. Excellent analytical skills specifically in program analysis requirements identification and structure. Stand ready to apply knowledge and acquired skills from previous education and work assignments. Managed multiple projects, met tight deadlines, and obtained quality results. Provide exceptional training, mentoring, coaching, and support to clients and colleagues.

AWARDS:
Meritorious Service Medal (2 awards)
Joint Service Commendation Medal (6 awards)
Army Commendation Medal (6 awards)
Army Achievement Medal (6 awards)
Joint Meritorious Unit Award
Meritorious Unit Citation (2 awards)
Army Good Conduct Medal (2 awards)
Army Reserve Component Achievement Medal
National Defense Service Medal (2 awards)
Afghanistan Campaign Medal (with campaign star)
Iraq Campaign Medal (with campaign star)
Global War on Terrorism Service Medal

FEDERAL TO GS-13: SECURITY SPECIALIST

> This applicant had extensive experience both in the federal sector, as well as the military prior to that, for a total of 30 years combined experience in law enforcement and criminal justice. The goal of this resume was to achieve a GS-13 position as a Security Specialist (Physical, Antiterrorism, Protection) or Supervisory Law Enforcement Specialist.

Gavin Thibadeaux
35567 Pinnacle Road
Port Sulphur, TN 55582 US
Day Phone: 123-456-7890 - Ext:
Evening Phone: 123-456-7890 - Ext:
Email: anyone@yahoo.com

Work Experience:
Department of Human Services Police Department
12 Skrillex Drive
Boston, IN   47324 United States

07/2015 - Present
Salary: 52,876.00 USD Per Year
Hours per week: 40
Series: 0083 Pay Plan: GS Grade: 6/10
Federal Police Officer (This is a federal job)

Duties, Accomplishments and Related Skills:
CRIME DETECTION AND COMPLIANCE ENFORCEMENT: Provide direction and oversight to three personnel with support to 5K employees, 3K patients, and families. Detect and prevent the occurrence of potential crimes and criminal activity in and around physical property. Investigate crimes that have occurred and any activity that may point to suspicious activity and arrest violators, informing them of their rights. Provide traffic control, issue citations, and assist people in emergency situations, including defense and protection. Enforce compliance of all local, state, and federal laws, to include ordinances, rules, and regulations, using various patrol procedures.

EMERGENCY AND SCENE MANAGEMENT: Respond to alarms and calls for assistance and question victims and witnesses at the scene; assist victims with medical needs. Take control of a scene and pursue, as necessary, those that resist. Respond to domestic disturbances and family disputes; report fire and safety hazards and take action, as required. Offer assistance to patients and visitors when called upon. Utilize defense, restraint, and nonlethal weapons with respect to offenders encountered. Gather information and statements pertaining to various scenes of assistance or other disturbance. Write reports that include relevant information and facts; classify reports and submit to proper channels in a timely manner according to procedure.

SUSPECT PROCESSING AND MULTIAGENCY COLLABORATION: Produce warrants at all levels when required and pertinent. Transport prisoners and suspects to and from assigned locations and facilities for in-processing into relevant databases and computer systems, including Automated Fingerprint Identification System (AFIS) and National Crime Information Center (NCIC). Collaborate with outside law enforcement agencies and make notification of relevant information with a need-to-know aspect of partnerships.

SECURITY IT APPLICATION: Apply Information Technology (IT) appropriately in typical daily tasks and to the production of effective security systems for the safety of all personnel working in the immediate facility and surrounding area. Used computers, radios, video equipment, mobile devices, GPS, and location assistance equipment, movement detection systems, and other technological tools and equipment. Exercised the three critical aspects of total security integration: personnel, physical, and information.

STRATEGIC PROGRAM MANAGEMENT: Formulated strategic program management and plans to aid in application of physical security programs. Implemented program and analyzed daily requirements with concurrence of threat conditions and general environmental mood. Injected risk assessment and mitigation techniques into daily activities to optimize protection capabilities for the whole of the installation. Resolved contingency adjustments in accordance with real and residual risk formulation partnered with applied technology.

SELECTED ACCOMPLISHMENTS:
*Collaborated in policy development for thousands of local cases up for judicial review; spearheaded procedure to produce more efficient and effective use of standard procedures to produce optimal results from seemingly ineffective and worn-out methodology.
*Proactively presented contemporary law enforcement methodology to entire department designed to produce more effective training, greater insight, and efficient time-saving techniques to improve tactics and procedures for long-term success.
*Advised leadership of cracks in the system of the NCIC; identified so-called "grey areas" in a procedure that might have been impeding progress in critical cases and the need for more specific information to produce a safer environment for patients and employees.

Shell County Sheriff's Department
88 Leeds Court
Misty Mountain, WV   48796 United States

03/2013 - 08/2015
Hours per week: 40
Reserve Sheriff Deputy

Duties, Accomplishments and Related Skills:
CRIME DETERRENCE AND RESPONSE: Provided direction and oversight to 3 personnel and supported a population of 50K people. Maintained presence in assigned locations with the purpose of preserving order and discipline, deterring crime, monitoring traffic violations, and enforcing laws, as appropriate. Responded to calls for assistance and evaluated the situation at arrival on scene. Implemented appropriate action, which included arrest, mediation, medical aid, or referral to corresponding outside agencies.

INVESTIGATION AND DOCUMENTATION: Investigated crimes, traffic accidents, fatalities, and minor violations; determined relevant information and contributing factors for crimes and minor incidents. Assembled information from all sources, including interviews, citations, arrests, use of force, and general disturbances; wrote reports documenting all relevant details and actions taken.

VENUE MANAGEMENT AND PATROL: Performed crowd control at public venues and gatherings, at special events, and during natural disasters. Maintained security at all times with assistance, as needed. Patrolled immediate vicinity with proximity to popular vacation destination to enforce maritime law and cite offenders for minor offenses.

ADMINISTRATIVE SUPPORT AND JUDICIAL PROCESS: Answered call to testify for court cases and judicial proceedings and administrative hearings; presented evidence and other valuable and relevant information. Served and executed legal paperwork for civil and criminal processes, search warrants, and arrest warrants; also served evictions and subpoenas and coordinated extradition activity. Provided corrections with direct contact and proximity to prisoners in County Jail facility.

SELECTED ACCOMPLISHMENTS:
*Donated personal time to a program designed to reduce the number of accidents at a popular vacation destination; partnered with full-time staff in support of special events and gatherings, eliminating accidents completely.

Civilian Police Department - U.S. Navy
Buena Vista Terrace
Encinitas, CA   97802 United States

01/2011 - 02/2013
Salary: 56,855.00 USD Per Year
Hours per week: 40
Series: 0083 Pay Plan: GS Grade: 10/3
Police Lieutenant/Watch Commander/Supervisor (This is a federal job)

Duties, Accomplishments and Related Skills:
PERSONNEL SUPERVISION, PLANNING, AND EVALUATION: Managed 25 personnel with oversight of 3 direct reports providing support to 2K people at the Marine Corps Mountain Warfare Training Center. Managed immediate assets worth $1.6M and held indirect responsibility for $3B. Planned and directed watch activities for assigned personnel. Supervised organizational operations in the absence of leadership. Conducted personnel evaluations and counseling, when necessary, and implemented corrective action, as required. Evaluated 25 personnel for training and performance standards and requirements.

ADMINISTRATIVE MANAGEMENT AND COORDINATION: Prepared morning reports and shift schedules, providing direction for the entire 24-hour period. Analyzed potential risk factors for various scenarios and developed physical security and force protection plans. Ensured continuity and compliance with pertinent policies, procedures, and local processes. Reviewed incident reports for each shift and acted appropriately. Maintained desk journals and confirmed accuracy of all submitted reports and paperwork. Maintained control of keys for assigned buildings and spot-checked cell blocks. Coordinated and issued equipment for specialized tasks and duties; issued assigned weapons for all personnel. Developed tasks and analyzed specific operations to increase efficiency and restructure procedures. Guided each shift with knowledge and enforcement of rules and regulations.

POLICING, DETECTION, AND SPECIAL PROCEDURES: Protected property and inhabitants while patrolling two individual facilities. Performed detection activities for various and potentially dangerous materials and scenarios, including bombs, drugs, and criminal activity. Utilized canine and electronic equipment for specialized detection procedures. Commanded Special Reaction Team (SRT); responded to volatile environments when called upon for robbery and domestic issues located in housing subdivisions. Implemented programs for Community-Oriented Policing and Problem-Oriented Policing; supervised throughout the department for law enforcement. Supervised investigations into various illegal actives and crimes. Monitored compliance with traffic laws and issued tickets in accordance with Uniform Code of Military Justice (UCMJ) and the Assimilative Crimes Act.

RESEARCH, INTERPRETATION, AND PROCEDURAL GUIDANCE: Researched police practices and procedures for contemporary implementation into organizational structure, including equipment, tactics, SRTs, mass casualty, and terrorist attacks. Interpreted Department of Defense (DOD) and Department of the Army (DA) security regulations, guidance, processes, and procedures and facilitated understanding and application in the performance of daily duties; ensured security policy compliance by all personnel under supervision.

TECHNICAL SECURITY APPLICATION: Applied a range of technical security concepts and principles to operational knowledge of electronic systems and testing equipment, to include surveillance and counter-surveillance equipment. Justified conflicts with best practices of radiofrequency (RF) and electromagnetic theory. Practiced regular use of a wide variety of equipment for radar operation, motion detection, and testing systems for optimal performance of policing functions.

SELECTED ACCOMPLISHMENTS:
*Identified need for increased expertise for assigned personnel through more consistent and exponentially more effective training; conducted and tracked critical requirements for 25 personnel, providing for incremental increases in overall effectiveness of policing tactics.
*Introduced analysis procedures for selective enforcement of specific violations ranging from tragic accidents to heinous sex crimes; identified criminal intelligence elements for proactive confinement and reduction in occurrences, resulting in a significant reduction in violent crimes and a 90% decrease in traffic accidents.
*Inserted Mobile Training Teams into training rotations to increase the intensity level and overall effectiveness of training opportunities; tracked and analyzed specific and recurring training scenarios and significantly reduced training costs by 50% for certifications and follow-on requirements.
*Trained an unprecedented 33% of department as drug recognition experts.
*Handpicked to oversee department during leadership absences; engaged staff and provided leadership necessary for continued operation of critical services for the local military community.

U.S. Army
Provincial Civil Support Team
Fallujah, Iraq, Al Anbar   Iraq

11/2007 - 12/2010
Salary: 100,000.00 USD Bi-weekly
Hours per week: 40
Captain/Military Police/Civil Affairs

Duties, Accomplishments and Related Skills:
PERSONNEL AND RESOURCE MANAGEMENT: Managed a Police/Civil Affairs team with responsibility for 180 personnel and direct oversight of 4 employees; provided support to 1.2M people in the immediate vicinity and managed $2.3M in resources, assets, and equipment. Liaised with relevant agencies, including the U.S. Department of State (DOS), U.S. Army, other federal entities, and the federal government; coordinated and developed critical infrastructure for security and law enforcement.

OPERATIONS MANAGEMENT AND POLICY COORDINATION: Managed designated funds of $2.3M for application to various and specialized operations; secured operations with training of foreign security agencies. Provided operations management for Military Police and Civil Affairs with designated entities and locations throughout the Area of Operations (AOO). Developed training of standards, policies, tactics, and techniques for foreign governments and national, provincial, and local police departments. Conducted hundreds of critical objectives in hostile territory.

TRAINING, DEVELOPMENT, AND INSTRUCTION: Monitored student/trainee progress for immediate training and long-term development requirements. Documented individual results and made recommendations for identified remedial and/or corrective action. Provided and supervised series of instructive mandates designed for optimal training results using specific teaching techniques, coaching methods, and basic mentorship through prepared lesson plans. Monitored progress through counseling, periodic reports, and testing. Participated in remedial instruction in various formats for students falling short of mandated standards.

TRAINING POLICY AND ACADEMIC IMPROVEMENT: Participated in development and revision of program materials; reviewed and analyzed lesson plans and modular training systems. Made recommendations for improvement to existing materials and suggested integration of relevant and contemporary information. Liaised with federal agencies, including U.S. Army, DOD, and DOS, as well as with U.S. criminal justice personnel and foreign nationals; collaborated in development of training policy and academic requirements, techniques, and procedures.

OPERATIONS SECURITY AND INVESTIGATIVE REPORTS: Produced clear and concise documentation and authored hundreds of investigative reports explaining the scope and results of technical, investigative, and operational endeavors; demonstrated lapses in security and intelligence pertaining to mission-critical activities. Managed Operations Security (OPSEC) programs, ensuring personnel participated in situational awareness for protection of sensitive/unclassified information. Adhered to OPSEC regulations with a Top Secret Single Scope Background Investigation clearance and managed intelligence personnel.

SELECTED ACCOMPLISHMENTS:
*Operated in hostile territory, completing 100+ dangerous missions in one year beyond the security and safety of identified boundaries; improved relationships with key leadership and civil operations, meeting with country and tribal leaders, improving critical friendly structure elements, and reducing insurgency in AOO.
*Provided mission-critical elements of funds management in support of area infrastructure and widespread improvements; projected and delivered monetary support with $2.3M, enabling reconstruction teams to provide long-term mission success and achievement of overall objectives.
*Organized and coordinated continual liaison with governmental agencies and area leadership to spearhead and encourage completion of assigned missions.
*Engaged key government leadership to evaluate and identify high-value targets through intelligence-gathering techniques; actions led to arrest of 12 known enemy leaders with significant and critical threat to allied forces throughout the region.

Education:
University of California San Diego, CA United States
Master's Degree 06/2015
GPA: 3.7 of a maximum 4.0
Credits Earned: 106 Semester hours
Major: Criminal Justice Administration
Relevant Coursework, Licenses and Certifications:
*Alpha Phi Sigma (Eta Theta Chapter) Honors Society
Foundations of Criminal Justice, 3 Sem Hrs; Contemporary Issues in Criminal Justice, 3 Sem Hrs; Criminology, 3 Sem Hrs;

Policing Theory and Practice, 3 Sem Hrs; Criminal Law, 3 Sem Hrs; Criminal Procedure, 3 Sem Hrs; Interpersonal Communication, 3 Sem Hrs; Criminal Court Systems, 3 Sem Hrs; Institutional and Community Corrections, 3 Sem Hrs; Criminal Organizations, 3 Sem Hrs; Juvenile Justice Systems and Processes, 3 Sem Hrs; Ethics in Criminal Justice, 3 Sem Hrs; Cultural Diversity in Criminal Justice, 3 Sem Hrs; Research Methods in Criminal Justice, 3 Sem Hrs; Organizational Behavior and Management, 3 Sem Hrs; Criminal Justice Administration, 3 Sem Hrs; Criminal Justice Policy Analysis, 3 Sem Hrs; Managing Criminal Justice Personnel, 3 Sem Hrs; Futures of Criminal Justice, 3 Sem Hrs; Survey of Justice and Security, 3 Sem Hrs; Organizational Administration, 3 Sem Hrs; Management of Institutional Risk, 3 Sem Hrs; Ethics in Justice and Security, 3 Sem Hrs; Criminological Theory, 3 Sem Hrs; Legal Issues in Security and Justice, 3 Sem Hrs; Critical Incident Management, 3 Sem Hrs; Cyber Crime and Information Systems Security, 3 Sem Hrs; Public Policy Issues, 3 Sem Hrs; Concepts of Physical and Personal Protection, 3 Sem Hrs; Forensic Science and Psychological Profiling, 3 Sem Hrs

University of Alaska Cicely, AK United States
Bachelor's Degree 09/2008
GPA: 3.81 of a maximum 4.0
Major: Cicely
Relevant Coursework, Licenses and Certifications:
Graduated with Honors

Job Related Training:
History of Law Enforcement, 04/2014; Constitutional Law, 04/2014; Civil Liability, 04/2014; Probable Cause, 04/2014; Search and Seizure, 04/2014; Community-Oriented Policing, 04/2014; Ethics in Law Enforcement, 04/2014; Cardiopulmonary Resuscitation (CPR), 04/2014; Crimes Against Persons, 04/2014; Domestic Violence/Stalking Investigations, 04/2014; Child Physical and Sexual Abuse, 04/2014; Crimes Against Property, 04/2014; Narcotics Laws and Investigations, 04/2014; Traffic Laws/Accident Investigations, 04/2014; Use of Force/Searches/Arrests/Defensive Tactics, 04/2014; Laws of Arrest, 04/2014; Patrol Procedures, 04/2014; Principles of Investigations, 04/2014; Collection and Preservation of Evidence, 04/2014; Firearms Training/Marksmanship, 04/2014; Unknown-Risk Vehicle Stops, 04/2014; High-Risk Vehicle Stops, 04/2014; Juvenile Law, 04/2014; Report Writing I, 04/2014; Active Assailant/Active Shooter, 04/2014; Building Searches, 04/2014; Crimes Against Elderly, 04/2014; Fingerprinting/Dusting for Latent Prints, 04/2014; Handling of Mentally Ill Persons, 04/2014; Report Writing II, 04/2014; Impact Weapons, 04/2014; Extraditions, 04/2014; Courtroom Demeanor/Giving Testimony, 04/2014; Jail Operations, 04/2014; Taser, 04/2014; Emergency Vehicle Operations/Pursuit Policy Review, 04/2014

Affiliations:
U.S. Army Military Police Officers Association - Member
Federal Law Enforcement Officers Association (FLEOA) - Member
American Federation of Government Employees - Member
U.S. Border Patrol Association - Former Member

Additional Information:
Hold Top Secret Sensitive Compartmented Information (TS SCI) security clearance

PROFESSIONAL SUMMARY:
Dedicated professional with 30+ years of Law Enforcement and Criminal Justice experience in civilian and military environments and with 20+ years and thousands of hours of training and instruction in classroom and hands-on methodology. Excels in suspect apprehension, with 5K+ arrests and significant contributions to overseas law enforcement and 200+ mis-

sions beyond the physical boundary of operations. Managed Operations Security (OPSEC) program and provided expert marksmanship instruction along with training in dozens of law enforcement and security tools and apparatus. Stand ready to provide law enforcement supervision and instruction for federal agency.

PROFESSIONAL HIGHLIGHTS:
*Conducted hundreds of critical objectives in hostile territory while implementing Counter-Insurgency Operations and Asymmetrical Warfare; in addition, performed responsibilities in training and foreign governmental infrastructure building.
*Performed 200+ military missions outside safety of installation security, providing patrols and expert verbal and written guidance for leadership elements, including host nation nationals during Operation Iraqi Freedom.
*5K+ arrests as sworn Law Enforcement Officer and Agent implementing full arrest authority in prevention, detection, apprehension, detention, and/or investigation of felony and/or misdemeanor violations of federal, state, local, tribal, or military criminal laws.
*Operated in 138+ countries around the world researching and analyzing technical threats directed toward U.S. intelligence community; utilized strategies to conduct Human Intelligence gathering and conduct counterterrorism operations against enemy threats.
*Managed OPSEC program for 20+ years, ensuring personnel participated in situational awareness in protection of sensitive/unclassified information.
*Army Marksmanship Instructor for basic pistol, shotgun, and M-16/M-4 rifle and a Close Quarter Combat/Close Quarter Battle (CQC/CQB) Instructor; Squad Designated Marksmanship (SDM) Instructor teaching 2,000+ personnel in 32 years of exemplary service.

AWARDS AND ACHIEVEMENTS:
*Achievement Certificates with Honors
*American Criminal Justice Association (ACJA) Award for Outstanding Scholastic Attainment
*Achievement Certificate in Law Enforcement Specialization (Honors)
*Achievement Certificate in Contemporary Police Technologies (Honors)
*Achievement Certificate in Investigations (Honors)

ADDITIONAL RELEVANT EXPERIENCE:
*Federal Protective Service Police (GSA), 2004-2007
*U.S. Border Patrol Agent (GS-1896-09/1), 2000-2004

PROFESSIONAL LICENSES AND CERTIFICATIONS:
*Federal Emergency Management Agency (FEMA) Incident Command System (ICS), 07/2015
*Commercial Driver's License, Class A, Combinations, Doubles/Triples, Tankers, Hazardous Materials (HAZMAT), 11/2014
*U.S. Federal Air Marshal (FAM), 02/2012
*Department of Public Safety, Louisiana P.O.S.T. Certified, General Law Enforcement Instructor, 02/2008

SPECIFIC QUALIFICATIONS:
Research and test a variety of state-of-the-art technical equipment and configured systems and advise leadership of the very latest technological advances; Maintain updated awareness of Department of Defense, U.S. Army Criminal Investigations Division, and Department of the Army (DA) along with other instructions, directives, and physical security policies relating to the performance of program missions; Apply Radiofrequency (RF) electromagnetic spectrum theory through understanding of wavelength conflicts and hazards and wavelength for use with detection; Certified for safety around the use of the X-ray, gamma ray, microwave, radar, RF, and sonic/laser/microwave motion detectors.

GS-11: LINGUIST/FOREIGN LANGUAGE INSTRUCTOR TRADITIONAL FEDERAL RESUME (FOR UPLOADING)

As a native of India, this applicant has a great deal of relevant experience as a linguist and cultural instructor through her work as a federal contractor and in the private sector. The resume is tailored using headlines, content, and keywords that reflected research, media, and political-analysis skills.

ROBIN GRANT

7744 Kaylor Circle, Apt. #5, Chevy, KS 56665 ▪ U.S. Citizen
Phone: 123-456-7890 mysite@gmail.com

VACANCY IDENTIFICATION NUMBER: xxxxx
JOB TITLE: Policy Analyst South Asia Region

PROFESSIONAL SUMMARY

Seasoned professional with more than 13 years of experience in international communications focused on U.S. relationships with South Asia. Seasoned agency delegate at the White House, United Nations, and Capitol Hill. Articulate communications expert with prodigious experience in written and nationally broadcast reporting, in both English and Hindi. Expert culture and language instructor who has developed innovative programs for the U.S. Department of State. Areas of expertise also include program management, event planning, strategic marketing, and professional networking. Now poised to leverage exceptional communication skills, cultural expertise, and vast knowledge of South Asian policy to help the U.S. Agency for International Development to meet and exceed its organizational goals.

RESEARCH & POLICY ANALYSIS: Expert researcher with extensive knowledge and understanding of South Asia, to include regional politics, jurisprudence, culture, economic development, security trends, U.S. interests, and human rights. Subject Matter Expert tasked with monitoring international media to follow events of political and cultural significance in South Asia, providing articulate analysis and interpretation of complex Hindi reports in English.

REPORTING & COMMUNICATIONS: Communications expert who has experience with national live broadcast reporting, interviewing prominent politicians, scriptwriting, drafting press releases, producing analytical annual reports, creating online presentations, and writing and publishing marketing materials. Distinguished linguist with oral fluency in English, Hindi, Urdu, and Punjabi. Well-spoken professional who produces superb work independently and is an effective team collaborator. Proven ability to multitask and work in a fast-paced setting, defining and meeting reporting deadlines.

REPRESENTATION: Articulate professional who has drafted Congressional testimony, addressed President Obama as a delegate at a White House briefing, and provided organizational representation at the United Nations and on Capitol Hill. Built and maintained extensive contacts in the U.S. and Asia with government officials, Non-Governmental Organizations, academia, and other organizations focused on freedom of religion or belief and related human rights.

"Her knowledge of U.S. Foreign Policy objectives in South Asia and expertise in socio-political situation in India was a huge advantage to our entire office. She put this skillset to work in order to deliver high-quality trainings to U.S. Foreign Service Officers." - CITED FROM RECENT PERFORMANCE EVALUATION

RELEVANT PROFESSIONAL EXPERIENCE

Language and Culture Instructor
U.S. Department of the Interior
333 Moneo Court
Washington, DC 22222
Hours/week: 40

02/2017 to Present
Salary: $72,800 USD Per Year
Supervisor: xxxxxx
Telephone: xxx-xxx-xxxx
OK to Contact: Yes

RESEARCH & POLICY ANALYSIS: Provide training to dozens of Foreign Service Officers (FSOs). Research and develop innovative comprehensive curricula as well as job-specific training plans. Monitor and analyze religious freedom conditions and related human rights as part of independent curriculum development and classroom instruction. Initiate and participate in analyses of complex cultural issues specific to South Asia with FSOs. Monitor and assess U.S. foreign policy and current affairs in South Asia to instruct and inform FSOs assigned to India. Monitor international media and reports and statements. Follow ongoing events affecting religious freedom or belief across South Asia.

AGENCY REPRESENTATION: Draft talking points for Program Director's Congressional testimony on instruction provided in the Near East Asia department. Work toward the inclusion of recommendations in U.S. government policies in India through cultural training of FSOs. Engage with White House and other federal agencies on issues relevant to South Asia.

TRAINING & INSTRUCTION: Develop innovative approaches to adult learning of Hindi language and culture, employing classroom techniques, education technology, and computer-based training. Apply education theories, principles, processes, and practices to develop training programs that meet diverse backgrounds and learning styles of adult students. Conduct individual and group training and instruction to further the achievement of individual and organizational goals. Research and observe classroom dynamics to inform curriculum development and make instructional recommendations. Develop extensive training documentation, including lesson plans, syllabi, and course outlines. Coordinate with team of seven personnel to develop weekly instructional plans to encompass all concurrent training requirements. Develop and execute lesson plans in compliance with weekly instructional plans to ensure program consistency and operational cohesion.

COMMUNICATIONS: Collaborate with seven personnel on long-term project to develop Hindi book for use as primary text for language instruction. Serve as Subject Matter Expert (SME) to interpret, analyze, and articulate complex Hindi articles in English. Effectively communicate with six personnel to edit instruction materials and ensure compliance with policy guidelines. Consult with South Asia Department Training Specialist to develop new courses and training methods to address varied learning styles and challenges. Engage students individually to analyze and respond to program challenges, provide language and cultural expertise, and make recommendations.

PERFORMANCE EVALUATION: Evaluate and report individual student progress in language and culture training programs with written and oral assessment tools. Deliver results and feedback directly to students throughout training programs. Obtain certification to administer and score official foreign language proficiency exams.

Select Value-Added Highlights:
*Prepared Congressional testimony talking points for Program Director on instruction provided in the Near East Asia department.
*Monitored international media for events affecting freedom of religion and issues of a political and cultural nature.
*Developed strategies and policy recommendations with FSOs to encourage improvement in the status of freedom of religion or belief in South Asia.
*Hand-selected to provide individualized training to the former Ambassador to India.

*Conceived and implemented immersion training program with rich cultural context, resulting in high-level language proficiency and cultural understanding for dozens of FSOs to date; program success led to development of parallel programs in other languages.

*Played critical role in overhaul of training curricula; independently developed four units of cultural curricula focused on consular services and topic-based language instruction.

*Recognized with two performance awards for innovative teaching approaches that elevated high standards in language training.

Asia Regional Manager	12/2015 to 01/2017
Shaping Lives	Salary: $45,000 USD Per Year
90 Aviary Road	Supervisor: xxxxx
Winchuck, NE 97336	Telephone: xxx-xxx-xxxx
Hours/week: 40	OK to Contact: Yes

PROGRAM MANAGEMENT: As Regional Manager for Asia, coordinated all aspects of sustainable development programs serving dozens of communities in India, the Philippines, and Indonesia. Supervised international staff, maintaining knowledge of unique regional politics, culture, and economic development of assigned countries in South Asia. Developed comprehensive agroforestry programs to promote sustainable development for countries in South Asia. Supervised remote staff of five managers and hundreds of personnel, located in assigned countries of India, the Philippines, and Indonesia. Oversaw implementation and sustainment of programs. Collected quarterly data from management team to provide quantitative and qualitative analysis of program effectiveness. Presented findings and recommendations to senior management. Oversaw budget development, requested disbursements, and monitored ongoing budgets for each program. Identified documentation and regulatory requirements of each program.

REPORTING: Drafted and ensured accuracy of annual reports on organization's programs in South Asia. Applied Strengths, Weaknesses, Opportunities, and Threats (SWOT) analysis to generate meaningful annual reports for organizations donors. Developed program profile for competitive non-profit funding platform, secured funding appointment, and submitted periodic project reports.

TRAINING & INSTRUCTION: Established training program for more than 300 personnel to provide step-by-step instruction for implementing sustainable development plans in South Asian countries at the community level. Provided program instruction and information on agroforestry methodology in both English and Hindi. Guided international staff on technical writing and oral communication to maintain consistent program messaging aligned with organizational objectives.

REPRESENTATION: Represented organization at a United Nations (UN) conference organized by the government of Bhutan; engaged in formal discussions of religious identity and presented organization's work and achievements to hundreds of conference attendees. Acted as chief liaison between in-country staff and U.S. headquarters, based on language proficiency and robust cultural knowledge of South Asia. Represented organization at various meetings and events that included official and unofficial foreign visitors and media.

COMMUNICATIONS: Drafted funding proposals for senior staff and donors based on research and needs assessments performed for each assigned country. Maintained multicultural relationships with senior management and executives in multiple countries. Collaborated with organizational development professionals to perform evaluations that informed management strategies throughout organization.

Select Value-Added Highlights:
*Published comprehensive annual reports, delivering SWOT analysis of sustainable development programs in South Asia.
*Represented organization at UN conference: engaged in formal discussions of religious identity and presented organization's work and achievements in South Asia to hundreds of conference attendees.
*Strategically reorganized Asia program; introduced new programs, expanded programming to additional countries, and sustained funding interests.
*Established program profile with prominent and competitive global crowdfunding platform, substantially increasing exposure to potential donors and securing sponsorship from more than 50 donors.

Marketing Associate/Marketing Manager	09/2012 to 11/2015
U.S. Pan Asian American Group	Salary: $45,000 USD Per Year
12 Aucklund Ave.	Supervisor: xxxxx
Washington, DC 55596	Telephone: xxx-xxx-xxxx
Hours/week: 40	OK to Contact: Yes

PROJECT MANAGEMENT: Coordinated strategic programming for nation's oldest and largest organization representing Asian Americans in business, sciences, the arts, sports, education, and community service. Expanded funding through corporate sponsorship and promoted organization's activities to diverse market segment of Asian-American business owners. Initiated multicultural marketing projects targeting Asian-American business owners that included special events and programs. Worked with team of up to five personnel to plan dozens of business procurement events as well as the largest annual Asian-American business conference in North America. Coordinated event registration and management. Developed comprehensive tiered sponsorship program that included multiple levels of sponsorship packages. Oversaw all events and activities for Asian-American division department. Organized, prepared materials, and provided logistical support for sustainable business trade mission to China and Taiwan, coordinating the work of two departments and corporate sponsors.

REPRESENTATION: Represented organization at high-level healthcare briefings and at various meetings and briefings targeting small and minority-owned businesses. Worked with personnel to address Congressional staff regarding interests of Asian-American businesses. Coordinated meetings, roundtables, and other events. Prepared materials for public events.

COMMUNICATIONS: Created strategic communications plan for outreach and growth among Asian-American business partners. Created outreach and event marketing flyers, brochures, and other materials. Served as liaison with Corporate department to coordinate business matchmaking services.

Select Value-Added Highlights:
*Established Asian-American business sponsorship program, fostering relationships and engagement with Asian-American businesses while setting organizational sponsorship record of more than $50K.
*Overcame language barriers to successfully coordinate sustainable business trade mission to China and Taiwan; coordinated logistical support for two departments and multiple corporate sponsors.

EDUCATION

Type and year of degree received:	Master of Science degree, 2014
Major field of study:	International Communication
College:	Schoolhouse University
Total Credits:	45
GPA:	3.65 out of 4.0

Thesis: "Language's Role in the National Identity of Postmodern India"; extensively researched India-Pakistan conflict over Kashmir from religious and cultural perspectives

Internships: External Communications, News Media
Relevant Coursework: Cross-Cultural Communication; Intercultural Communication; International Communication; Special Topics in International Politics - Dialog Approaches; Quantitative Analysis in International Affairs; Conflict Analysis and Resolution - Theory and Practice; Organizational Communications; Negotiations; Special Institute in International Affairs - Religion and Culture in Conflict; Extensive research on and analysis of India-Pakistan conflict over Kashmir from a religious perspective

Type and year of degree received: Bachelor of Science degree, 2008
Major field of study: Mass Communication
College: Anywhere University
Total Credits: 81

Relevant Coursework: Communication Theory, Research, and Evaluation; Communicative Language; Multimedia Tools and Technology; Traditional Methods of Entertainment for Adult Education; Photography and Audiovisual Production; Film, Video and TV Production; Scriptwriting; Audio Engineering; Social and Linguistic Theories and Approaches; Critical Theory of Media and Language; Advanced audiovisual documentary project focused on Tibetans exiled in India for religious beliefs

OTHER QUALIFICATIONS

CAREER-RELATED TRAINING
Fluency in reading and writing Hindi (native language)
Fluency in conversational Urdu and Punjabi

Internship with Save the World International, 2015; Prepared organizational newsletter and provided fundraising and conference support for non-profit organization with a mission to reduce human suffering working with 19 countries across Asia, Africa, and the Middle East. Basic French Certificate Course, 2010

PROFESSIONAL PUBLICATIONS:
Grant, Robin, S., (2014) "Improving National Happiness." Forestry Journal.

JOB-RELATED HONORS & AWARDS:
-Multiple performance awards for innovative language instruction techniques.
-Guest Lecturer on Mass Communication Theory and Approaches

COMPUTER SKILLS:
Microsoft (MS) Windows; MS Office (Word, Excel, Access PowerPoint, Outlook); MS SharePoint; MS Publisher; Adobe Photoshop, PageMaker, and InDesign; Final Cut Pro; Rosetta Stone

SAMPLE COVER LETTER

DANIEL BERGERON
123 South West Street Jackson, MS 88549
Home Phone Number: 123-456-7890
Work Phone Number: 223-559-5547
Email: anyname@gmail.com

September 5, 2018

Office of Counsel
Office of Inspector General
U.S. Department of Commerce
1401 Constitution Avenue, NW
Washington, DC 20230

Dear Hiring Manager:

I am writing you in response to the vacancy announcement: 8885-RD-519, Attorney Advisor, GS-905-11. My experience and expertise providing legal advice and services on a wide variety of civil, criminal and administrative legal issues, including fraud, contract law, federal disclosure statements, ethics, employee standards of conduct, Equal Employment Opportunity, and other Human Resources matters. I have also worked in a variety of legal environments, including judicial courts, law firms, and federal agencies such as Equal Employment Opportunity Commission (EEOC).

Prior to law school graduation, I served in a variety of law clerk, teaching, and advocacy positions. As a Law Clerk for the EEOC, I conducted legal research on civil and criminal issues and drafted memoranda on topics such as Title VII, Discrimination Employment Act, and Affirmative Action. During my General Practice Clinic, I represented a criminal client successfully and advocated for clients in substandard housing.

I earned my Juris Doctor degree from the University of Maryland in 2016, demonstrating academic excellence by graduating in the top third of class. After graduation from law school, based on my judicial expertise, I was selected for a highly prestigious clerkship with the Alabama Court of Special Appeals. In this role, I have researched and drafted numerous, precedent-setting opinions in a variety of areas, including contract law, employment law, family law, class actions, fraud, and criminal law.

I am currently a member of the State Bar in Alabama, and my expertise in providing legal advice and advocacy would be an immediate asset to your organization. I would appreciate your serious consideration, and look forward to hearing from you soon.

Sincerely,

Daniel Bergeron

USEFUL LINKS AND RESOURCES

HR University: the federal government's "one-stop" training resource center for the federal Human Resources (HR) pro.
https://hru.gov/index.aspx

CareerPro Global
http://www.careerproplus.com

SES Writers
http://www.seswriters.com

Pathways program explanation
https://hru.gov/Studio_Recruitment/Job_Seekers_Resource_Center.aspx

General Schedule (GS) Position Classifications
https://www.opm.gov/policy-data-oversight/classification-qualifications/classifying-general-schedule-positions/occupationalhandbook.pdf

Federal Compensation Scales
https://www.opm.gov/policy-data-oversight/pay-leave/salaries-wages/2017/general-schedule/

USAJOBS Help Page
https://www.usajobs.gov/Help/

O*Net (U.S. Department of Labor)
http://online.onetcenter.org/

Federal Job Descriptions
http://www.opm.gov/fedclass/html/gsseries.asp

U.S. Department of Labor Occupational Handbook
https://www.bls.gov/ooh/

Office of Personnel Management
http://www.opm.gov/

Wage Grade Job Classifications
http://www.opm.gov/fedclass/html/fwseries.asp

ECQ Information

https://www.opm.gov/policy-data-oversight/senior-executive-service/executive-core-qualifications/#url=Overall-Chart

FEDmanager
http://www.fedmanager.com/

Military Skills Translator
http://www.military.com/skills-translator/mos-translator

DOD Dictionary of Military Terms
http://www.dtic.mil/doctrine/dod_dictionary/

Military Lexicon
http://www.fas.org/news/reference/lexicon/lexicon.htm

Veteran's Service Records (U.S. National Archives)
http://www.archives.gov/veterans/military-service-records/

Veterans' Employment and Training Service Regional Office Contacts http://www.dol.gov/vets/aboutvets/contacts/main.htm#RegionalStateDirectory

U.S. Department of Education Accredited Postsecondary Institutions and Programs
http://www.ope.ed.gov/accreditation/

RESUME ACTION VERBS

Accelerate	Calculate	Correct
Accentuate	Capitalize	Corroborate
Accomplish	Capture	Counsel
Accommodate	Catalog	Craft
Achieve	Catapult	Create
Acquire	Centralize	Critique
Adapt	Champion	Crystallize
Address	Change	Curtail
Adjudicate	Chart	Cut
Advance	Clarify	Decipher
Advise	Classify	Decrease
Advocate	Close	Define
Align	Coach	Delegate
Alter	Collaborate	Deliver
Analyze	Collect	Demonstrate
Anchor	Command	Deploy
Apply	Commercialize	Derive
Appoint	Commoditize	Design
Appreciate	Communicate	Detail
Arbitrate	Compare	Detect
Architect	Compel	Determine
Arrange	Compile	Develop
Articulate	Complete	Devise
Ascertain	Compute	Differentiate
Assemble	Conceive	Direct
Assess	Conceptualize	Discern
Assist	Conclude	Discover
Augment	Conduct	Dispense
Authenticate	Conserve	Display
Author	Consolidate	Distinguish
Authorize	Construct	Distribute
Balance	Consult	Diversify
Believe	Continue	Divert
Bestow	Contract	Document
Brainstorm	Control	Dominate
Brief	Convert	Double
Budget	Convey	Draft
Build	Coordinate	Drive

Earn	Finance	Inventory
Edit	Forge	Investigate
Educate	Form	Judge
Effect	Formalize	Justify
Effectuate	Formulate	Launch
Elect	Foster	Lead
Elevate	Found	Lecture
Eliminate	Gain	Leverage
Emphasize	Generate	License
Empower	Govern	Listen
Enact	Graduate	Locate
Encourage	Guide	Lower
Endeavor	Halt	Maintain
Endorse	Handle	Manage
Endure	Head	Manipulate
Energize	Hire	Manufacture
Enforce	Honor	Map
Engineer	Hypothesize	Market
Enhance	Identify	Master
Enlist	Illustrate	Mastermind
Enliven	Imagine	Maximize
Ensure	Implement	Measure
Entrench	Import	Mediate
Equalize	Improve	Mentor
Establish	Improvise	Merge
Estimate	Increase	Minimize
Evaluate	Influence	Model
Examine	Inform	Moderate
Exceed	Initiate	Modify
Execute	Innovate	Monetize
Exhibit	Inspect	Monitor
Exhort	Inspire	Motivate
Expand	Install	Navigate
Expedite	Institute	Negotiate
Experiment	Instruct	Network
Explode	Integrate	Nominate
Explore	Intensify	Normalize
Export	Interpret	Obfuscate
Extricate	Interview	Observe
Facilitate	Introduce	Obtain
Finalize	Invent	Offer

Officiate	Provide	Respond
Operate	Publicize	Restore
Optimize	Purchase	Restructure
Orchestrate	Purify	Retain
Organize	Qualify	Retrieve
Orient	Quantify	Reuse
Originate	Query	Review
Outsource	Question	Revise
Overcome	Raise	Revitalize
Overhaul	Rate	Sanctify
Oversee	Ratify	Satisfy
Participate	Realign	Schedule
Partner	Rebuild	Secure
Perceive	Recapture	Select
Perfect	Receive	Separate
Perform	Recognize	Serve
Persuade	Recommend	Service
Pilot	Reconcile	Shepherd
Pinpoint	Record	Simplify
Pioneer	Recruit	Slash
Plan	Recycle	Sold
Position	Redesign	Solidify
Predict	Reduce	Solve
Prepare	Reengineer	Spark
Prescribe	Regain	Speak
Present	Regulate	Spearhead
Preside	Rehabilitate	Specify
Process	Reinforce	Standardize
Procure	Rejuvenate	Steer
Produce	Remedy	Stimulate
Program	Render	Strategize
Progress	Renegotiate	Streamline
Project	Renew	Strengthen
Project Manage	Renovate	Structure
Proliferate	Reorganize	Study
Promote	Report	Substantiate
Propel	Reposition	Succeed
Propose	Represent	Suggest
Prospect	Research	Summarize
Prove	Resolve	Supervise

Supplement

Supply

Support

Surpass

Synergize

Synthesize

Systematize

Tabulate

Target

Teach

Terminate

Test

Thwart

Train

Transcribe

Transfer

Transform

Transition

Translate

Trim

Troubleshoot

Unify

Unite

Update

Upgrade

Use

Utilize

Verbalize

Verify

Win

Work

Write

ACCOMPLISHMENTS WORKSHEET

JOB INFORMATION:
(You might want to write in your job title, start and end dates, and any other information to help you be organized for when you develop your resume.)

_____

_____

_____

TOP DUTIES:

1. _____

2. _____

3. _____

4. _____

5. _____

6. _____

7. _____

8. _____

TOP RESULTS/ACCOMPLISHMENTS:

1. _____

_____

2. _____

_____

3. _____

_____

4. _____

_____

5. _____

_____

6. _____

_____

7. _____

_____

8. _____

_____

JOB INFORMATION:
(You might want to write in your job title, start and end dates, and any other information to help you be organized for when you develop your resume.)

_____

_____

_____

TOP DUTIES:

1. _____

2. _____

3. _____

4. _____

5. _____

6. _____

7. _____

8. _____

TOP RESULTS/ACCOMPLISHMENTS:

1. _____

_____

2. _____

_____

3. _____

_____

4. _____

_____

5. _____

_____

6. _____

_____

7. _____

_____

8. _____

_____

JOB INFORMATION:
(You might want to write in your job title, start and end dates, and any other information to help you be organized for when you develop your resume.)

_____

_____

_____

TOP DUTIES:

1. _____

2. _____

3. _____

4. _____

5. _____

6. _____

7. _____

8. _____

TOP RESULTS/ACCOMPLISHMENTS:

1. _____

_____

2. _____

_____

3. _____

_____

4. _____

_____

5. _____

_____

6. _____

_____

7. _____

_____

8. _____

_____

JOB INFORMATION:
(You might want to write in your job title, start and end dates, and any other information to help you be organized for when you develop your resume.)

_____

_____

_____

TOP DUTIES:

1. _____

2. _____

3. _____

4. _____

5. _____

6. _____

7. _____

8. _____

TOP RESULTS/ACCOMPLISHMENTS:

1. _____

_____

2. _____

_____

3. _____

_____

4. _____

_____

5. _____

_____

6. _____

_____

7. _____

_____

8. _____

Roadmap to Federal Jobs Worksheet

Instructions: This worksheet is designed to use each time you apply for a federal job. It's best to follow the checkpoints in order, and don't move on until you complete all the steps in a given checkpoint. Once you apply for a job and begin preparing for the interview, simply go back to checkpoint 1 and start again with your next application. Cast a wide net and follow the best practices in the book, and you should eventually find the perfect federal job for you! And remember, you can always refer back to the Roadmap to Federal Jobs book for more detailed information in each area.

Check Point 1 — Select a Starting Point

List Federal Agencies and Jobs of Interest:

_____

_____

_____

_____

Check Point 2 — Determine Your Qualifications for a Specific Job

Write the Job Title/Agency _____

Did you review the duties?   Y   N

Will you be able to show your experience/abilities in your resume?   Y   N

Did you review the special qualifications and/or KSAs?   Y   N

Will you be able to demonstrate your experience in these areas?   Y   N

Check Point 3 — Develop your Federal Resume

Did you identify keywords/headlines/themes?   Y   N

Did you integrate those into your resume?   Y   N

Did you optimize the Additional Information section?
Y   N

Did you edit your resume and check character counts?
Y   N

Check Point 4 — Develop Knowledge, Skills and Abilities (KSA) Statements

Does the job require KSA essays or mini-KSAs?   Y   N

Did you write them?   Y   N

Check Point 5 & 6 — Apply for the Job, Follow Up, and Interview Prep

Did you read the job again from top to bottom?   Y   N

Did you review the closing date, how to apply, and required documents?   Y   N

Did you Post Your Resume on USAJOBS.gov?   Y   N

Did you complete the Occupational Questionnaire?   Y   N

Write the date you applied & the job title and #

_____

_____

Did you receive written and/or verbal confirmation?   Y   N

Have you prepared for the interview?   Y   N

Did you follow up after two, four, and/or eight weeks?   Y   N

Write down dates of follow up: _____

_____

USAJOBS

INFORMATION QUESTIONNAIRE/OFFLINE RESUME BUILDER

YOUR PERSONAL INFORMATION	
	Enter your information below in these blocks:
First Name:	
Middle Name:	
Last Name:	
Home Address:	
Home Address 2:	
City:	
State:	
Zip Code:	
Country:	
Email Address:	
Day Phone:	
Evening Phone:	
Mobile Phone:	
DSN (if applicable):	
Are/were you a Federal Civilian Employee?	
If so, enter Pay Plan (e.g., GS, WG, ST, etc.):	
Enter Series:	
Enter Grade:	
Federal Civilian Employee Start Date:	
Federal Civilian Employee End Date:	

YOUR EMPLOYMENT

Need information for each job **for the past 10 years (approximately)**
Begin with your most recent job first
Required fields are in RED, but enter as much information as possible
Add additional work information to <u>ADDITIONAL INFORMATION</u> at the end of this document if necessary

EMPLOYMENT BLOCK ONE (most recent)	
Employer Name:	
Employer Address:	
Employer Address 2:	
City/Town:	
State/Province, Zip Code:	
Country:	
Formal Title:	
Start Date (MM/YYYY):	
End Date (MM/YYYY):	
Salary:	
Average Hours Per Week:	
May we contact your supervisor?	
Supervisor's Name: (only if contact answer is Yes)	
Supervisor's Phone: (only if contact answer is Yes)	
Pay Plan-Series-Grade: (only if Federal civilian position)	

DUTIES/SCOPE OF RESPONSIBILITY AND SPECIFIC ACCOMPLISHMENTS: (5,000 char.)

Create your keyword-rich headlines below, and organize relevant position description/core duties, and other related information in these headlines. Remember to include "nuts and bolts" information such as number of people supervised directly, how many customers/organizations you supported, and how much money/resources you managed. Next, include your top 3-5 accomplishments for this position.

HEADLINE:

HEADLINE:

HEADLINE:

HEADLINE:

SELECTED ACCOMPLISHMENTS:

EMPLOYMENT BLOCK TWO	
Employer Name:	
Employer Address:	
Employer Address 2:	
City/Town:	
State/Province, Zip Code:	
Country:	
Formal Title:	
Start Date (MM/YYYY):	
End Date (MM/YYYY):	
Salary:	
Average Hours Per Week:	
May we contact your supervisor?	
Supervisor's Name: (only if contact answer is Yes)	
Supervisor's Phone: (only if contact answer is Yes)	
Pay Plan-Series-Grade: (only if Federal civilian position)	

DUTIES/SCOPE OF RESPONSIBILITY AND SPECIFIC ACCOMPLISHMENTS: (5,000 char.)

Create your keyword-rich headlines below, and organize relevant position description/core duties, and other related information in these headlines. Remember to include "nuts and bolts" information such as number of people supervised directly, how many customers/organizations you supported, and how much money/resources you managed. Next, include your top 3-5 accomplishments for this position.

HEADLINE:

HEADLINE:

HEADLINE:

HEADLINE:

SELECTED ACCOMPLISHMENTS:

EMPLOYMENT BLOCK THREE	
Employer Name:	
Employer Address:	
Employer Address 2:	
City/Town:	
State/Province, Zip Code:	
Country:	
Formal Title:	
Start Date (MM/YYYY):	
End Date (MM/YYYY):	
Salary:	
Average Hours Per Week:	
May we contact your supervisor?	
Supervisor's Name: (only if contact answer is Yes)	
Supervisor's Phone: (only if contact answer is Yes)	
Pay Plan-Series-Grade: (only if Federal civilian position)	

DUTIES/SCOPE OF RESPONSIBILITY AND SPECIFIC ACCOMPLISHMENTS: (5,000 char.)

Create your keyword-rich headlines below, and organize relevant position description/core duties, and other related information in these headlines. Remember to include "nuts and bolts" information such as number of people supervised directly, how many customers/organizations you supported, and how much money/resources you managed. Next, include your top 3-5 accomplishments for this position.

HEADLINE:

HEADLINE:

HEADLINE:

HEADLINE:

SELECTED ACCOMPLISHMENTS:

EMPLOYMENT BLOCK FOUR	
Employer Name:	
Employer Address:	
Employer Address 2:	
City/Town:	
State/Province, Zip Code:	
Country:	
Formal Title:	
Start Date (MM/YYYY):	
End Date (MM/YYYY):	
Salary:	
Average Hours Per Week:	
May we contact your supervisor?	
Supervisor's Name: (only if contact answer is Yes)	
Supervisor's Phone: (only if contact answer is Yes)	
Pay Plan-Series-Grade: (only if Federal civilian position)	

DUTIES/SCOPE OF RESPONSIBILITY AND SPECIFIC ACCOMPLISHMENTS: (5,000 char.)

Create your keyword-rich headlines below, and organize relevant position description/core duties, and other related information in these headlines. Remember to include "nuts and bolts" information such as number of people supervised directly, how many customers/organizations you supported, and how much money/resources you managed. Next, include your top 3-5 accomplishments for this position.

HEADLINE:

HEADLINE:

HEADLINE:

HEADLINE:

SELECTED ACCOMPLISHMENTS:

EMPLOYMENT BLOCK FIVE	
Employer Name:	
Employer Address:	
Employer Address 2:	
City/Town:	
State/Province, Zip Code:	
Country:	
Formal Title:	
Start Date (MM/YYYY):	
End Date (MM/YYYY):	
Salary:	
Average Hours Per Week:	
May we contact your supervisor?	
Supervisor's Name: (only if contact answer is Yes)	
Supervisor's Phone: (only if contact answer is Yes)	
Pay Plan-Series-Grade: (only if Federal civilian position)	

DUTIES/SCOPE OF RESPONSIBILITY AND SPECIFIC ACCOMPLISHMENTS: (5,000 char)

Create your keyword-rich headlines below, and organize relevant position description/core duties, and other related information in these headlines. Remember to include "nuts and bolts" information such as number of people supervised directly, how many customers/organizations you supported, and how much money/resources you managed. Next, include your top 3-5 accomplishments for this position.

HEADLINE:

HEADLINE:

HEADLINE:

HEADLINE:

SELECTED ACCOMPLISHMENTS:

EDUCATION BLOCK ONE	
School or Program Name:	
City/Town:	
State/Territory/Province:	
Country:	
Degree/Level Attained:	
Completion Date (MM/YYYY):	
Major:	
Minor:	
GPA:	of GPA Max.:
Total Credits Earned:	
Semester or Quarter Credits?	
Honors:	

RELEVANT COURSEWORK, LICENSURES AND CERTIFICATIONS
(list the titles and completion month/year)
Enter below:

JOB RELATED TRAINING

(list the titles and completion month/year of training courses/certifications relevant to the position)

Enter below:

REFERENCES	
List up to 5	
Name:	
Employer:	
Title:	
Phone:	
Email:	
Reference Type:	Personal or Professional? (client to select online)

Name:	
Employer:	
Title:	
Phone:	
Email:	
Reference Type:	Personal or Professional? (client to select online)

Name:	
Employer:	
Title:	
Phone:	
Email:	
Reference Type:	Personal or Professional? (client to select online)

Name:	
Employer:	
Title:	
Phone:	
Email:	
Reference Type:	Personal or Professional? (client to select online)

ADDITIONAL INFORMATION (up to 20,000 char.)

- **Security Clearance** (list any active or previous security clearances, relevant dates and certifying agency)

- **Professional Summary** (You may want to include a short paragraph that describes your professional experience and skills.

Here is a simple formula for writing a good professional summary:

1. An introductory statement displaying your highest level of qualifications and Number of years of work experience: Be specific: "Senior maintenance supervisor with 27 years of progressive experience."
2. Record of improvement/accomplishment: Whenever describing accomplishments, be precise. If possible, quantify results. For example, you could write, "Reorganized order processing procedures to reduce time required by 30%."
3. Specific skills and training applicable to the job objective.
4. Areas of specialized proficiency (include education level, specialized certifications, and/or security clearances).
5. Work ethic traits demonstrating desirable behaviors or competencies (keep this to one sentence)

- **Career Highlights** (here, you can simply copy/paste some of your top accomplishments from throughout the resume. If these include keywords from the job announcement, all the better!)

- **Additional Relevant Experience** (if you have positions going back past 10 years that you think are relevant, you can list the start and end years, the job title, and the organization here. You may also want to include a summary of your duties/accomplishments. Finally, if you ran out of space in the work history above, you might want to continue them here is you really think it's relevant)

- **Honors, Awards and Recognition** (list the name and month/year received for awards)

- **Military Awards** (list highest awards such as medals and war zone deployment ribbons, but not other badges such as weapons training, good conduct, airborne, etc. unless they are relevant to the job)

- **KSAs** (if the position requires to you include KSAs in the resume, this is a good place to include them.)

- **Performance/Rater Comments** (consider listing short excerpts of others who wrote about your performance. If possible, choose quotes that are relevant to the position.)

- **Professional Affiliations** (list the organization name and affiliation – only include current memberships or position held)

- **Equipment/Tools/Systems**

- **Speaking Experience**

- **Publications** (list any relevant professional journal articles or books you wrote that were published)

- **Areas of Expertise** (Soft Skills such as communication, speaking, and teambuilding- and Technical Skills such as computer or other technology skills. This is yet another opportunity to include some relevant keywords from the job announcement.)

KSA WORKSHEET

This worksheet will help you to write your responses to any KSA (Knowledge, Skills, and Abilities) essay statements.

List KSA Here: _____

Your Topic or Example: _____

CHALLENGE: Describe a specific problem or goal and the obstacles, problems, and challenges you faced in achieving your goal.

_____

_____

_____

CONTEXT: Title of your job or role you are playing in this example. Talk about the individuals and groups with whom you worked and/or the environment in which you worked, to tackle a particular challenge.

_____

_____

_____

_____

ACTION: Discuss the specific actions you took to address a challenge. Describe your role and actions in resolving the problem or meeting the outcome goals.

_____

_____

_____

_____

RESULT: Describe results, outcomes, or long-term impacts of your efforts.

_____

_____

_____

_____

CD CONTENTS

Worksheets and Customizable Samples:

- ✔ Accomplishments Worksheet
- ✔ Cover Letter Sample
- ✔ KSA Worksheet
- ✔ Roadmap to Federal Jobs Worksheet
- ✔ Traditional Federal Resume Template (for uploading)
- ✔ USAJOBS Resume Builder

Resume Samples:

- ✔ Federal GS-13: Aviation Safety Inspector
- ✔ Federal GS-13: Security Specialist
- ✔ Military to GS-5: Human Resources
- ✔ Military to GS-7: Veterans Service Representative
- ✔ Military to GS-12: HR Specialist/Program Analyst
- ✔ Military to GS-12: Intelligence Analyst
- ✔ Military to GS-15: Supervisory Program Management
- ✔ Private Sector to GS-7: Dental Hygienist
- ✔ Private Sector to GS-9: Program Specialist
- ✔ Private Sector to GS-11: Linguist/Foreign Language Instructor
- ✔ Private Sector to GS-15: Land/Property Management
- ✔ Private Sector to WG-12: Aircraft Mechanic

I'm sure you guys appreciate feedback on how your products work out. I just wanted to let you know that it's been one month since I got my new resume from you and I already have two interviews scheduled for awesome jobs, including the stretch position of Washington State Forester that I started this whole effort. The other is the Director of Forest Management for The Nature Conservancy. This has been an awesome experience and I just wanted to say thank you. --Brad, 2018

Once again, your company defines customer service. Your expertise in this line of work is unmatched. The attention to detail and wordsmith that you perform is the reason I decided to reach back out. The service is always amazing and always get(s) the job. I can always count on you getting it done on the first try. Thank you. --R.G., 2018

I found the process to be an engaging and rewarding experience! I learned a lot, and I really enjoyed collaborating/partnering with my writer, William "Bill" Carroll! He provided an excellent final product, one that was nicely formatted, written very well, and exceptionally communicated cherrypicked highlights of my experience and accomplishments. Standing out amongst the crowd should not be an issue! --R.R., 2018

Honestly, my experience with CareerPro has been exceptional, the process streamlined and efficient. The career adviser was very helpful during the consultation, and the writer went above and beyond to make sure every section of the resume reflected my professional and military experience. The end result was a resume I'm very proud of and [landed] me a job. --L. Bryant, 2018

From the first consultation, to the hand off, to the first draft, and final draft the communication and back and forth feedback was first rate. I was a little apprehensive from sticker shock when I first got the quote but I am glad I went the route. My cover letter and resume reads very well and my writer did a great job of whittling down what I would call a complex work history and highlighting the pertinent elements in a two-page document. I will gladly recommend your service to anyone especially the many service members I come in contact with. Thank you once again. I can tell you have a great company atmosphere

and a real importance placed on customer service! --J. Cuddy, 2018

I would highly recommend these guys to anyone who wanted help building their own professional federal resume. The price you pay for it is well worth the cost and the finished product proves it. They are not only extremely knowledgeable about everything it takes to create your masterpiece. They are extremely nice, professional, patient, and highly efficient. They work incredible hours to help make sure they get everything from you, that is needed and correct. Then create the most beautiful picture of your entire career. Thank you to my writer and his team for all their expertise, time, and help. --J. Dienes, 2018

I've been working my entire life for the private sector, but decided to pursue federal employment. I applied for several positions without having received an interview using the resume I wrote. I decided to change my approached and have my resume professional written for a federal employer. I give CareerPro Global A++ rating; the professional resume writer was fantastic, he was very responsive, he understood my experience and wrote my resume toward to the position I was interested. He did a great job and I totally recommend their services. --J.C., 2018

Just wanted to let you know that because of your work developing my SES application, I had my interview today with DIA. Add another to a success in getting the interview. Thanks to you and the team! You do great work and I will recommend CareerPro to others. --Chris, 2018

CareerPro Global
YOUR CAREER IS OUR BUSINESS®

careerproplus.com – seswriters.com – militaryresumewriters.com
1-800-471-9201

After serving more than 60,000 clients over the past three decades, we can assist you with:

Resume Writing for:
- Private Sector to Federal
- Federal to Federal
- Federal to Private Sector
- Military to Federal
- Military to Private Sector
- Private Sector to Private Sector

SES Application Coaching & Development - Resume, ECQs, and TQs

Interview Preparation

Expert Training, Consulting, and Coaching:
- Onsite USAJOBS resume workshops (or webinars)
- Tailored presentations, workshops, webinars, etc., to meet agency needs
- Online ECQ Writing Courses
- SES Application and ECQ Editing/Coaching
- Award Justifications
- Writing Effective CCAR Accomplishments and Narratives

careerproplus.com – seswriters.com – militaryresumewriters.com
1-800-471-9201

After serving more than 60,000 clients over the past three decades, we can assist you with:

Resume Writing for:
- Private Sector to Federal
- Federal to Federal
- Federal to Private Sector
- Military to Federal
- Military to Private Sector
- Private Sector to Private Sector

SES Application Coaching & Development - Resume, ECQs, and TQs

Interview Preparation

Expert Training, Consulting, and Coaching:
- Onsite USAJOBS resume workshops (or webinars)
- Tailored presentations, workshops, webinars, etc., to meet agency needs
- Online ECQ Writing Courses
- SES Application and ECQ Editing/Coaching
- Award Justifications
- Writing Effective CCAR Accomplishments and Narratives